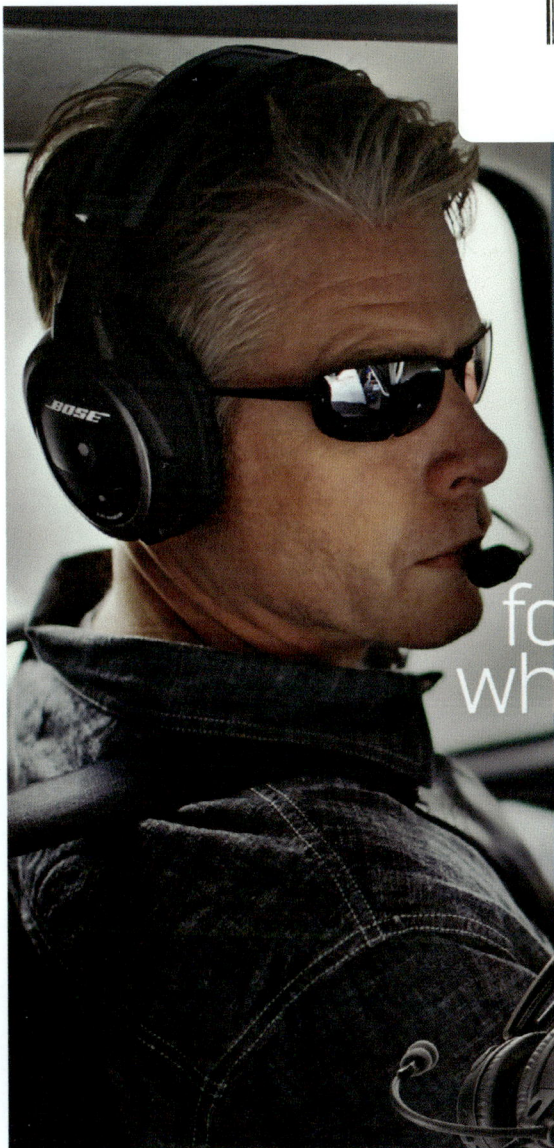

I like to stay ahead of my airplane. So if I'm 40 miles out with weather rolling in, I'm listening to what's happening in front of me. ATIS. Pilot chatter. A quick check with flight service. Sometimes, there's a lot to decipher. But I need to hear it clearly. Because when I do, I feel confident. Prepared. In the moment. And that allows me to just

focus on
what matters,
flying.

Bose® A20®
Aviation Headset

Bose Aviation Europe
Noise Reduction Technology Group

Nijverheidstraat 8
1135 GE Edam
The Netherlands
Web: http://Global.Bose.com
E-mail: Aviation_Europe@Bose.com
Tel.: +31 (0)299 390 777

MORE NOISE REDUCTION.
LESS DISTRACTION.

Better sound can make all the difference, especially where you go. Which is why, with 30% greater noise reduction than conventional noise reducing aviation headsets, the A20® headset lets you hear more of what you need to hear. While proprietary cushions and minimal clamping force let you fly comfortably for hours. Meets or exceeds TSO standards.

FAA TSO and ETSO C139 Certified. ©2013 Bose Corporation.

CW01425770

Udo Leinhäuser

AVIATOR'S GUIDE TO

Florida

SEAIR VERLAG

Udo Leinhäuser
AVIATOR S GUIDE TO FLORIDA

PUBLISHER
Seair Verlag GmbH & CO KG
Am Goldbichl 13
D-82054 Sauerlach

MAIL & INTERNET
info@aviators-guide.com
www.aviators-guide.com

PHOTOS
Udo Leinhäuser (except for pages 29, 30, 31, 32)

LAYOUT AND DESIGN
Melanie Ellmers-Ost
www.meodesign.de

TRANSLATION
Leinhäuser Language Services GmbH
www.l-ls.com

Reproduction or further electronic use, including excerpts, permitted only with prior written approval from the publisher.

1st English edition December 2013

ISBN-10: 1493504428
ISBN-13: 978-1493504428

Dear Readers,

The Aviator's Guide to Florida is the solution to a problem that we editors at *fliegermagazin* know only too well. For most pilots, it is easy to find the navigational information needed to fly to an unknown destination. Official publications, sectional charts, websites all help you to quickly plan your flight route and time and contain information such as airfield operating hours and fuel availability. However, it gets more difficult when tourist information is requested. What do we do once we get to our destination? How do you get from the airfield to a new place or plan a day trip that is not only interesting for the pilot, but also family and friends? Looking for a restaurant near the airfield is usually the first priority after landing in a new area – tourist attractions, places worth visiting and transport options to get there are the next most important pieces of information. And it can be difficult to come by.

Because we have to address exactly these issues in our flight magazine "fliegermagazin," which is the largest monthly German-language magazine for general aviation and flight topics, the Aviator's Guide to Florida is perfect for us and for our readers. Author Udo Leinhäuser has filled a critical information gap in the only way possible: He went to Florida and did all the research himself – with an airplane. He has gathered a wealth of information, tips and recommendations from local pilots there. Of course, the Aviator's Guide also includes important basic flying information. However, more interesting are the recommendations that Udo Leinhäuser provides on what to do once you've landed. After all, Florida is an east coast state that is easy to get to and a sun-drenched dream destination for European and American pilots alike. The weather is almost always perfect for flying, general aviation costs are much lower than here in Europe and its multitude of attractions offers something for everyone. Let the Aviator's Guide inspire you and guide you – fliegermagazin wishes you happy reading during flights around Florida!

Editor-in-chief for *fliegermagazin*

Thomas Borchert

INTRODUCTION

Flying in Florida is like skiing in the Alps, surfing in Hawaii or scuba diving in the Caribbean. Either you've done it already - or it's definitely on your bucket list. This book is intended to aid you in quickly finding Florida's most beautiful destinations. Lonely beaches, beautifully maintained golf courses, impressive countryside and inspiring cities: Florida has something for everyone. It also has a lot to offer in terms of flying: from quiet airfields in the back country to dense air space in greater metropolitan areas. Pilots of all levels and experience will have no problem finding exciting and interesting destinations.

The first section of the guide describes the history of Florida as well as providing useful information on flying in American air space.

The main sections of the guide are split up geographically into North, Central and South Florida.

Here you will find information on the individual flight destinations. There is also a wealth of information provided for every airfield or local airport, starting from what to look out for when landing, recommendations for local tourist activities along with a lot of photos. Detailed information on each airfield is provided in the information boxes on the left side.

| R W Y | Runway dimensions and, if applicable, glide slope indicators. |

Important frequencies

Air traffic density at the field

Fuel supply

SERVICES

Under Services, we have provided information on the topic of transport as well as other useful information on the airfield.

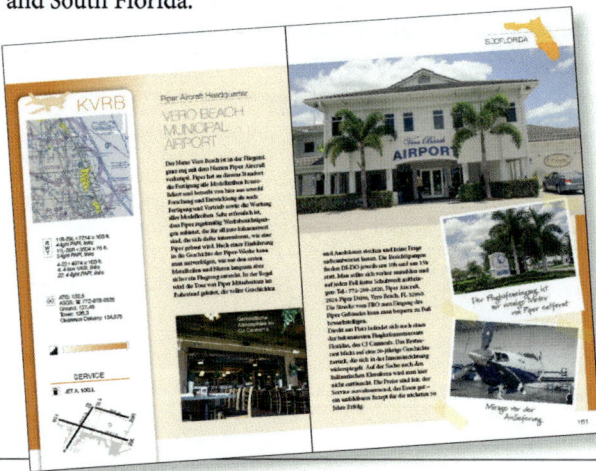

This information is in no way sufficient for complete flight planning - more on this below - rather, it mainly provides a decision-basis for selecting a travel destination.

The information regarding the air traffic volume at the airfield or local airport should be taken with a pinch of salt because air traffic is naturally

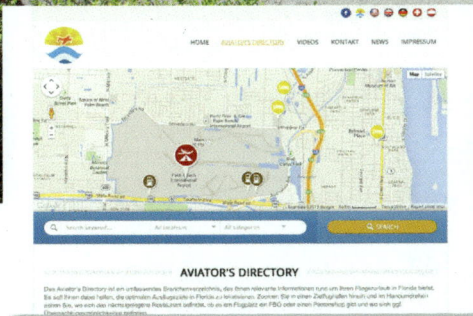

AVIATOR'S DIRECTORY

subject to heavy fluctuations, depending on day of the week or time of day. However, the information provided here should at least serve as a starting point for calculating how much air traffic to expect at the destination airport. My goal is to share with as many pilots as possible the beauty of Florida as well as the perks to flying in this state. That is why this book also very purposefully caters to non-American pilots who have never flown in the USA before. It is for these pilots that the Aviator's Guide also contains a good deal of flying information, much of which is a given for US-based pilots. I hope this book makes it easier for many foreign pilots who come to Florida for flight training or a flyers' holiday to enjoy the flying paradise that is Florida.

I have made every effort to gather the most interesting selection of day trip destinations, restaurants and recreational activities on the ground as possible.

However, this list is in no way exhaustive. For more information, please refer to the **"Aviator's Directory"** www.aviators-guide.com. In addition to a multitude of additional information, the **"Aviator's Directory"** also includes feedback from other visitors and customers. Simply zoom-in to your preferred destination airport on the map and see what's available there. Or write a review yourself based on your last visit. Check it out! It's worth the visit. I hope that this book provides you with useful information on planning your flyers' holiday in Florida. If, despite thorough research and in-depth review, you find errors, I would be happy to receive any feedback under info@aviators-guide.com.

Have fun flying in Florida and here's wishing you a soft landing always!

Best regards,

Udo Leinhäuser

CONTENT

NORTH FLORIDA

CENTRAL FLORIDA

CONTENT

SOUTH FLORIDA

AVIATOR'S GUIDE TO FLORIDA

FOR MORE INFORMATION
AND TIPS ON TRAVEL

WWW.AVIATORS-GUIDE.COM

FLORIDA AND ITS HISTORY

▪ Introduction

Florida can look back on a rich history with many important events that have had a broad impact on American history as a whole. Due to its geographical location as a hub between the northern and southern hemisphere, Florida has always been a setting that has attracted diverse external influences but also suffered intense internal conflicts. Its history has brought together the destinies of many different groups of peoples, from the Native Americans and African Americans to the European settlers and Latin American immigrants. It is a stage where the fates of young and old, rich and poor, winners and losers play out. The streams of tourists, migrants and immigrants to Florida have had a far-reaching impact on the state, whether in terms of military or social conflicts or important technological achievements, but have made Florida what it is today. Florida has experienced unimaginable changes at an inconceivable speed. Only by tracing the many different threads of historical events in Florida's past can you truly understand modern Florida.

▪ Florida's Native American Population

Traces of Florida's pre-historic past go back at least 14,000 years. Archeological findings from the Paleoindian Period have been found near sinkholes and karst limestone basins, which, at that time, were the source of fresh water and now form the beds of Florida's modern rivers. Around 8000 B.C., the climate in Florida was warmer and more humid due to the melting glaciers. At the same time, the sea level rose, the landmass sank, and with it, probably any signs of early coastal cultures. The rising volumes of water supported population growth and nurtured the development of the Early Archaic culture, which left behind many archeological footprints at numerous sites around the panhandle. A prominent example of these early settlements is the Windover Pond archeological site in Brevard County, near Titusville.[1] Additional permanent settlements from the Middle Archaic Period (roughly 5000 B.C.) were found near wetlands that were inhabited for many generations. In the Late Archaic Period (about 3000 B.C.), settlers lived both in freshwater as well as saltwater wetlands and helped change the landscape with their growing settlements, earth mounds and archaic shell rings. A good example of these can be found on Horr's Island on the south end of Marco Island in Collier County.[2] In the period around 500 B.C., findings have shown the development of strongly fragmented and independent regional cultures.[3] Post-Archaic cultures in eastern and southern Florida evolved in a relatively isolated

way. They were heavily dependent on the fertile eco-system of the river delta regions, but these cultures were not agricultural by nature. In contrast to the south and east, the northern areas of Florida were notice-ably influenced by the Mississippi culture, which flourished between about 800 A.D. and 1500 A.D. as well as two indigenous cultures: the Pensacola culture (about 1100 - 1700 A.D.)[4] and the Fort-Walton culture (about 1200 - 1500 A.D.). These two cultures relied heavily on corn cultivation, built platform mounds for ceremonial, po-litical and religious purposes and were also familiar with various methods of pottery. This way of life was probably adapted from the Mississippi culture.[5]

When the first Spanish explorers arrived at the beginning of the 16th century, the number of indigenous inhabitants in Flo-rida was estimated at 350,000. The Spanish records indicate about 100 known native tribes, which were highly distinctive from one another, especially in their political organization. For example, some Apalachee native tribes were organized perfectly as one political entity in several regions. Other Apalachee settlements, in contrast, did not nurture political relationships with one another. The Timucua people, made up of many diverse tribes with roughly 150,000 members, spoke different dialects of the Timucua language. Despite having a common language, these tribes had very different cultural traditions.[6]

The first explorers to arrive on Florida shores came into contact with many other indigenous tribes, such as the Ais, Alafay, Amacano, Calusa, Jojoro, Mayaimi, Tocobaga, Uzita and many others. Some of the tribes were only mentioned in passing and had only sporadic contact with the Spanish explorers, while other tribes were described in great detail. Many native Americans integrated into the Spanish missions in Florida. Toward the end of the 18th century, however, many of the tribes were in danger of extinction. The main reason for this was the infectious diseases brought over from Europe - smallpox and measles, to name a few - which the native American immune system was not equipped to fight. Secondly, the military conflicts with the Spanish and English and, finally, slavery, which was introduced by the Spanish in the 16th century, and later, by the English and their Indian allies, were also contributing factors. In the end, only a few Apalachee tribes were able to retreat to Louisiana, where their descendants still live today. When Florida became a part of the British Empire in 1763, a small number of survivors from different native tribes immigrated, together with the Spanish, to Cuba and New Spain (Mexico). During the 18th century, the Seminole tribes themselves established a new ethnic group made up of the different tribes of Native Americans, mostly Creek. They stayed away from European settlers and their descendants, which helped them survive. Today, three of

these tribes are federally recognized in the USA as official ethnic groups: the Seminole Nation of Oklahoma,[7] the Seminole Tribe of Florida[8] and the Miccosukee Tribe of Indians of Florida.[9]

From Colony to State

■ The First Spanish Rule (1513-1763)

After Christopher Columbus completed his first journey across the Atlantic under the patronage of the Spanish royal family, awareness of the New World spread throughout Europe. New opportunities and potential riches attracted many people to travel to the New World. They were even encouraged by European monarchies who wanted to expand their kingdoms through colonization and the acquisition of raw materials.

Juan Ponce de León led a Spanish expedition that set sail from Punta Aguada, Puerto Rico, on March 3, 1513, and eventually led to the discovery of Florida. He had been a member of Columbus' second expedition and was already considered an experienced explorer. The Spanish crown had appointed him the first governor of Puerto Rico. Ponce de León reached the east coast of the panhandle on April 7 during the Spanish

ABOVE Juan Ponce de León
LEFT Ponce de León discovers Florida
(wood cut)

Easter celebration. That's why he named this new region, La Pascua de la Florida, after the traditional Catholic name for Easter. According to later reports, Ponce de León was mainly motivated by the search for a "fountain of youth," which indigenous stories spread around the peninsula.[10] It is possible that previous Spanish explorers had already reached Florida because at least one native spoke Spanish in 1513. However, further evidence for this could not be found.[11]

After this first discovery, several attempts to explore the peninsula and establish settlements failed. The second expedition led by Ponce de León landed in 1521 near the Caloosahatchee River or at Charlotte Harbor, with a group of about 200 settlers and their domestic animals. The expedition was attacked by the Calusas tribe and driven away. During the attack, Ponce de León was hit in the shoulder by a poisoned arrow. He died shortly thereafter in Havana, Cuba.

In 1528, Pánfilo de Narváez landed in Rio de las Palmas – known today as the "Jungle Prada Site" in St. Petersburg. After already losing half of his men at sea, he was met on land by hostile natives. His weakened troops marched northwards to the territory of the Apalachee tribes without finding any gold or other treasures. His attempt at colonization also failed. He decided to return to Spain, but it was too late,[12] Pánfilo de Narváez died in Florida, side by side with most of the members of his expedition.[13]

In another attempt to explore the Florida panhandle, Hernando de Soto set out in May 1539 with a large-scale expedition consisting of nine ships and 620 men, landing in what is now Bradenton, which he named Espíritu Santo. Thanks to Juan Ortiz, who he hired as the leader, Soto's expedition was at least a partial success. Ortiz, the only survivor of

RIGHT Pedro Menéndez de Avilés (1519–1574), Spanish Admiral and first Governor of Florida

PEDRO MENENDEZ DE AVILES.
Natural de Aviles en Asturias, Comendador de la orden de Santiago, Conquistador de la Florida, nombrado Gral. de la Armada contra Inglatierra. Murio en Santander A. 1574 á los 55 de edad.

the Narváez expedition, was held captive for many years by the natives and had learned how to communicate with them. Ortiz led the expedition with the help of another guide, Perico, who spoke several of the local languages. Their success was due to the effort they made to contact the local tribes in advance in order to avoid hostilities. The expedition was able to push northward and explore the west coast of the peninsula.[14] Another early Spanish settlement also succeeded in gaining a foothold in Pensacola. Tristán de Luna y Arellano arrived in 1559 with the intention of conquering Florida. He succeeded in establishing a colony which, however, had to be abandoned in 1561 after being destroyed by a hurricane.[15] The attempt to settle the region was not pursued again for 135 years because it was considered too dangerous.[16] Even the French Huguenots tried their luck in Florida. In 1564, René Goulaine de Laudonnière reached the delta of the May River (St. Johns River) and sailed upstream. There he founded Fort Caroline – today's

Jacksonville – where many Huguenots found protection from religious persecution.[17] The colony fought to survive when Pedro Menéndez de Avilés arrived in the name of Spain's King Phillip II to drive the French out of Florida. In September 1565, the Spanish attacked Fort Caroline under Menéndez de Avilés and killed most of the Huguenot settlers. However, the French succeeded in winning back Fort Caroline from the Spanish in 1567.

In the middle of the military conflict with the French, Menéndez de Avilés founded St. Augustine in 1565. It was meant to be the first successful Spanish settlement on the continent and an influential city in the region for 300 years.[18] St. Augustine withstood numerous attacks over the years until it was finally destroyed by Englishman Sir Francis Drake in 1586. From their base in St. Augustine, Catholic missionaries successfully controlled their remote dependents. By 1655, they had converted roughly 26,000 natives to Catholicism.

During the 17th century, St. Augustine survived revolts, epidemics and pirate attacks. Yet the Spanish foothold there loosened. English settlers from the north pushed the Spanish further south while the French settlers along the Mississippi crossed into the western borders of the Spanish territory. In 1702, St. Augustine was attacked by the English Colonel James Moore who had formed an alliance with the Indian tribes. However, he was not successful in gaining control of the settlement. The English subsequently attacked the Spanish missions, executed the converted natives and finally brought the Catholic missions to their knees. With the defeat of the Apalachee-tribe in 1704, which was allied with the Spanish during the Queen Anne war, the native population was also decimated. Between 1715 and 1717, many native American refugees fled to southern Florida after the Yamasee war. In 1719, the French were finally able to bring the Pensacola settlement under their control.[19]

African slaves held by the British further north were drawn to the Spanish settlements in Florida as escape destinations, which created a major point of contention between the British and Spanish colonists who were constantly at war with one another. Once the slaves reached Spanish territory, they could gain their freedom if they converted to Catholicism. Many former slaves settled in a community two miles north of St. Augustine called Gracia Real de Santa Teresa de Mose, which was the first settlement of freed African slaves in North America. Other communities of native Americans, such as the Creek and the Seminoles, also took in slaves who had escaped to the Spanish territory. This incensed British government representatives,[20] leading the British to successfully conquer St. Augustine in 1740.

■ The British Rule (1763-1783)

Then, in 1763, Spain worked out an agreement with Britain to trade Florida for control over Havana, which the British had lost during the Seven Years' War. The majority of the Spanish left Florida and took a large part of the native population with them to Cuba.

The British divided the peninsula into East and West Florida and began a campaign to attract settlers to the new colony. Scottish physician Dr. Andrew Turnbull founded the colony New Smyrna (Volusia County) in East Florida.

When the British moved the border further north into what is now Mississippi and Alabama in 1767, the Creek native tribes

Seminole Chief Osceola (1804–1838)

in the south moved to Florida and there established the Seminole tribe.[21]

During the American War of Independence, both regions of Florida sided with the British when the colonies declared their independence. The overwhelming majority of Floridians at that time were loyalists and even supported attacks in the American south.

In 1781, Spain regained control of Pensacola from Britain. Then, two years later, at the end of the war, Spain regained Florida through the Treaty of Paris, which ended the War of Independence.[22] Because the peace treaty did not define borders and the Spanish attempted to expand their territory, this created a conflict with the United States, which, in turn, was finally settled in the Treaty of San Lorenzo.[23]

■ The Second Spanish Rule (1783-1821)

The Second Spanish Rule showed that the country's foothold had been weakened. The uncontrolled territory became an escape destination for runaway slaves as well as for insurgent natives who routinely attacked the United States from Florida. Spain's lack of presence and its power vacuum were used by the American settlers who began to move into the Spanish territory and make it their own. Also, the British settlers under Spanish rule took advantage of the situation. They instigated a rebellion and assumed control of the Spanish garrison in Baton Rouge. There, on September 23, 1810, they declared it the "Free and Independent Republic of West Florida".[24]

In 1810, the President of the United States, James Madison, declared the annexation of parts of West Florida which he believed to be included in the Louisiana Purchase of 1803, and incorporated them with the Orleans territory.[25] Furthermore, the USA annexed the Mobile district of West Florida in 1812 and joined it with the Mississippi territory.[26] Spain objected to the takeover of its territories but, due to its weakened position, was powerless and had to make do with ruling the rest of its colony from Pensacola.

In the meantime, the US army grew in strength in the area and undertook several military campaigns in the Spanish regions of East Florida. From there, the Seminole Indians initiated repeated attacks on settlers in Georgia. Between 1817-1818, the US army, under the command of Andrew Jackson, fought the First Seminole War against the Seminole Indians.[27] Spain's weakened position and the conflict with the Seminoles finally led to the de-facto control over East Florida by the USA. Florida had thus become a burden for Spain. Because Spain could not afford to regain control over its colony, it handed it over to the United States in 1812.[28]

■ From Territory to Statehood Florida (1822-1845)

The Florida territory was incorporated into the United States on March 30, 1822 as an "organized territory."[29] East Florida and what was left of West Florida were joined together and Tallahassee became the chosen capital. New settlers came in and established additional farming colonies and plantations. Colonists and Seminoles were constantly in conflict over the fact that the Seminoles gave protection to runaway slaves. So the settlers put pressure on the government to drive the Seminoles out of Florida. In the Treaty of Paynés Landing (1832), the US government promised the Seminoles land west of the Mississippi in exchange for their

voluntary resettlement. The majority of the Seminoles left the territory, some, however, stayed and prepared to fight for their land. The settlers continued pressuring the government to drive out all of the Seminoles. The result was the Second Seminole War,[30] which was triggered by the Dade massacre.[31] Under the leadership of Chief Osceola, the Seminoles attacked two US company troops totaling 110 soldiers from the rear on December 28, 1835 and left only one soldier alive.

The victory encouraged the Seminoles to continue their attacks against the US troops. The army fought for seven years repeatedly against the native tribe. The war finally ended in 1842 with roughly 1500 deaths in the military and an unknown number of dead white civilians, Seminoles and African-Americans. About 4000 Seminoles were deported from Florida to the Indian territory belonging to the Creek tribe. This awakened resentment in their leaders in Florida. Some Seminoles remained in the Everglades area and avoided contact with the white settlers. On March 3, 1845, Florida became the 27th state of the United States of America. At this time, the white settlers had already established large cotton and sugar cane plantations with the help of the enslaved African-Americans. The remaining Seminoles were forced by the army patrols from Fort Myers to leave the region. This led to animosities and an attack on the fort by the Seminoles: This was the trigger for the Third Seminole War

(1855-1858).[32] And at the end of the war, the surviving Seminoles were forced to leave their lands. Only a very few remained in the Everglades. They remained extremely unobtrusive and kept themselves isolated from the rest of the population.

African-Americans in Florida

■ The American Civil War

After Abraham Lincoln was elected as US president, Florida ceded from the Union, along with other southern states, on January 10, 1861. Together, these states founded the Confederate States of America. During the resulting Civil War, the army of the confederate states was heavily dependent on supplies from Florida. The Union army took advantage of this and tried to set up a blockade through the state by gaining control of its most important ports, including Cedar Key, Jacksonville, Key West and Pensacola. However, Florida's long coast made this strategy very difficult.[33]

In 1860, Florida had 140,424 inhabitants, 44 % of whom were slaves.[34] During the war, many slaves escaped from the southern plantations located in regions under Union control. The Union encouraged the slaves to flee and then hired them as soldiers or sailors or as spies against the confederate troops. As the war continued, rumors of a slave revolt grew louder and the confederate army began to show weakness. Many deserters joined together to form bands that led attacks against the confederate troops.

In May 1865, a Union division was ordered to regain control of the federation through Florida. Shortly thereafter, the last active Confederate troops surrendered to the Union troops. As part of a ceremony celebrating Lincoln's reading of the Declaration of Independence in Tallahassee, slavery was officially abolished in Florida on May 20, 1865.

■ Reconstruction und Disenfranchisement

After meeting the requirements of Reconstruction, Florida re-entered the Union on July 25, 1868. [35] The goal of Reconstruction was to give the secessioned states the opportunity to regain their political self-determination and a seat in Congress as well as assuring the former leaders of the Confederate states and freed slaves their civil status. These policies triggered far-reaching protests and discussions in all southern states, including Florida. The 15th Amendment to the Constitution protected the rights of former slaves to vote and was ratified, after much debate, in 1870. It prevented states from refusing

Slaves dance to banjo music, "The Old Plantation" from the late 18th century

a male citizen the right to vote based on race or color or previous condition of slavery or involuntary servitude. Reconstruction also officially gave the former slaves the same constitutional rights to vote and to hold public office.

However, in 1877, the southern white Democrats succeeded in regaining their political dominance. This was due, in part, to the aggressions demonstrated by the white paramilitary groups that intimidated the former slaves and prevented them from exercising their right to vote. Between 1885 and 1889, laws were passed in Florida, under the leadership of the southern white Democrats, that created barriers for blacks and poor whites to vote. The southern white Democrats were thus able to reinforce their control in the single-party state, without any opposition.[36]

Without the right to vote, African-Americans were not allowed to sit on a jury or assume other public offices. The southern Democrats went even further by passing the Jim Crow laws,[37] which enforced the segregation of blacks and whites in all public areas in the former confederate states.

This segregation and discrimination was practiced at all levels of southern society: in public schools, public buildings, public transport, bathrooms, restaurants and separate drinking fountains. The situation continued for over 60 years. With Congress under the control of the southern Democrats, African-Americans were politically under-represented until 1966.

By the end of the 19th century, Florida's population was mainly made up of white Protestants from the south who were farmers or plantation owners. In 1900, Florida had 529,000 inhabitants, 43.7% of whom were African-American.[38]

■ Great Migration (1910-1940)

Racially motivated violence against African-Americans was a daily occurrence in the first half of the 20th century in the southern states of the US. The black population was not only not allowed to vote, it was also segregated and disenfranchised on every level socially due to the Jim Crow laws. Furthermore, blacks and black communities frequently suffered violent attacks, such as the Rosewood Massacre,[39] during which blacks were murdered, their houses and churches destroyed. After the First World War, a wave of self-administered justice rolled over the state.

Violence, racial segregation and inequality of opportunity triggered a wave of migration from the southern states, particularly in the deep south, to the "Black Belt, " northern and western cities such as New York, Chicago, Philadelphia, St. Louis, Detroit, Pittsburgh, Cleveland and Indianapolis. There, black migrants found better jobs – in the steel and meatpacking industries and in the slaughterhouses – better schools, and black men were allowed to vote. Roughly 40,000 African-Americans left Florida between 1910 and 1940.[40]

■ The Civil Rights Movement

Between 1954 and 1968, the organized battle to end discrimination against African-Americans intensified, especially in southern states. In the 1940's and 50's, many African-Americans fought for civil rights. The "G.I. Bill" gave many veterans of the Second World War the opportunity to pursue further education and to own homes, as well as offering further advantages that were intended to facilitate their re-entry back into civilian life and to climb the social ladder. These rights increased the call for equal rights for African-Americans who had also fought in the war against Nazi Germany. Social tensions escalated between 1951-52, resulting in a wave of bomb attacks by the Ku Klux Klan against activists.

The Sunshine State as Tourist Destination

Florida's appeal as a tourist destination evolved as early as the 19th century. Henry Flagler [41] – industrialist and founder of Standard Oil – developed the Florida east coast and later laid the cornerstone for the Florida East Coast Railway from Jacksonville to Key West. He built the Ponce de León Hotel in St. Augustine, which opened in 1888.[42] The hotel's success awakened his interest in making further investments and developing the east coast. To make the southern tip of the panhandle more accessible, he had a railway bridge built over the St. Johns River and purchased the Hotel Ormond near Daytona. In addition to other major projects, Flagler also founded Palm Beach and West Palm Beach in 1894. There, he built the Royal Poinciana Hotel with 1100 rooms and later the Palm Beach Inn – which is now called Breakers Hotel.[43] His tourism projects were accompanied by railroad expansion. Cold weather fronts hit

Henry Morrison Flagler

ABOVE Henry Morrison Flagler (* born January 2, 1830 in Hopewell, New York; † May 20, 1913 in West Palm Beach, Florida)

LEFT Henry Flagler House

the Palm Beach region in 1894 and 1895, leading him to continue his development activities further south. In the Miami area, Flagler was offered a land deal by landowner and businesswoman Julia Tuttle who wanted the deal to push the expansion of the railroad network further south. Flagler developed the region's infrastructure, building road networks as well as water and power utilities. In 1896, the railroad made it to the tip of the panhandle in Biscayne Bay. There, Flagler opened the luxury Royal Palm Hotel in 1897. He supported fruit tree planting and harvest along the rail lines and promoted the construction of hospitals, churches and schools throughout the entire state. Ultimately, he is considered the "Father of Miami."

Even before the founding of Disney World, Florida had theme parks. The beaches and Florida's image as paradise on Earth were the main attractions for vacationers. Working American families were able to afford a vacation in Florida. The successful marketing of the "Sunshine State" regularly attracted Americans who mostly traveled there by

car. Commerce along the roads flourished, with the construction of gas stations, diners and motels for tourists. In 1955, Delta Airlines made getting to Florida attractive for many and flew tourists to new destinations in lesser developed beach regions. The Botanical Gardens in the center of St. Petersburg, the so-called Sunken Gardens,[44] was an important tourist destination in the 1930's. With the natural attractions of Silver Springs[45] and Weeki Wachee Springs,[46] tourists were able to experience and marvel at the native animal world on land, from glass-bottomed boats and even the underwater performances by women dressed up as mermaids. The most well-known attraction in the period between 1950 and the opening of Disney World was Cypress Gardens,[47] famous for its water ski performances and gardens as well as the Southern Belles. Marineland,[48] one of Florida's first parks for sea mammals, became a famous attraction and well-known as the world's first "Oceanarium." Nevertheless, Miami and Miami Beach became Florida's greatest tourist magnets. Vacationers were fascinat-

ABOVED & LEFT Weeki Wachee Springs State Park, Florida
RIGHT Sunken Gardens in St. Petersburg

ed by the exclusivity and the "touch of sin" that surrounded these cities.

At the end of the 1960's, tourist spending in Florida had reached $1 billion dollars annually.[49] But tourists were still segregated by race, ethnic group, class, age and religion. What was affordable for some, was inconceivable for others. Signs like "Whites only", "For none-Jews only," or "No Mexicans" were normal, depending on the establishment. Despite the fact that a law prohibiting discriminating signs like this had been in place since 1955, Anti-Semitism in Miami and Miami Beach was widespread well into the 1960's. In the exclusive resorts, blacks were working poorly paid service jobs and also had to carry ID cards with them, to distinguish them from potential undesirable intruders. But there were also black tourists. The legendary Jazz and Blues clubs of the 1950's attracted guests in droves. There were also holiday resorts only for African-Americans. The most popular destination for blacks was American Beach on Amelia Island. The few Seminoles who still lived in the Everglades learned to take advantage of the tourism boom. With the opening of the Tampa-Miami rail route in 1928, which ran through the Everglades, tourists traveled down from the north and got to know the "true" wilderness of the Indian villages and learned to value the lifestyle that went with it. The Seminole understood how to attract the masses of tourists traveling through their region with typical scenes of "Indian life." Ironically, after hundreds of years of poverty, the Seminoles today are among the wealthiest tribes. About $27 billion in revenue are earned by the tribal gambling

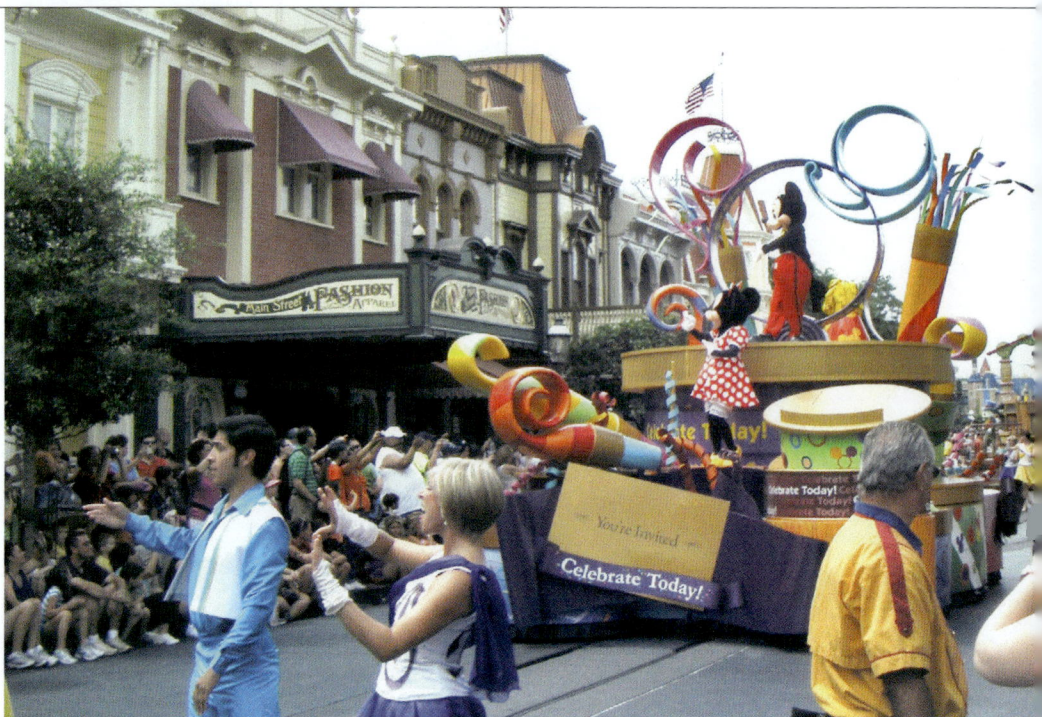

industry, of that $2.16 billion in gambling.[50] Yet nothing changed the tourist industry in Florida more than the opening of Disney World in 1971. Disney World raised the bar in Florida's tourism industry and redefined the word "fantasy." A new fantasy world was created based on nostalgic photos and the most modern technologies as well as a new kind of tourism experience that was designed and controlled right down to the last detail. For this undertaking, Disney purchased land equal to the size of Manhattan, which consisted mainly of forest and swamp areas. As a private corporation, Disney held the extraordinary power to define for itself the environmental, policing and tax policies as well as land use for Disney World. After its opening, in the first year alone, 11 million tourists made the trip to Disney World. In 1982, the EPCOT (Experimental Prototype Community of Tomorrow) Center

opened. By 1990, it was drawing about 10 million visitors annually. With the addition of Disney/MGM Studios in 1989 and Disney Animal Kingdom in 1998, millions more visitors flocked to the region. In 2012 all Walt Disney Parks together recorded roughly 50 million visitors.[51]

If this wasn't enough, Orlando also built another money-making theme park. In 1973, SeaWorld[52] opened its doors to the public. Universal Studios Florida[53] opened in 1990 and recorded 5.9 million visitors in 2012. Tourists spend $17 billion annually at these five mega parks in Orlando, which employ 66,000 workers.[54] The Orlando International Airport was expanded accordingly and had 35 million travelers passing through its gates in 2010.

The mega theme parks have had an enormous impact on Florida's economy. The once small shops on the beach that served

ABOVE LEFT Tree Of Life
at Disney's Animal Kingdom
LEFT Cinderella Castle at Magic Kingdom -
Walt Disney World Resort, Orlando, Florida

Land Speculation in Florida

Florida's population skyrocketed in the 20th century. Around 1900, Florida was more of a rural society with a population of 529,000. However, in 2010, the Florida census had counted 18.8 million inhabitants: 60.1 % Whites, 17 % African-Americans, 2.1% Asian Americans, 1.4 % other (Indians) and the remaining 18% were Hispanic Americans or Latinos.[56] While the population in the neighboring southern states dropped in the 1920's, the number of people living in Florida rose by half a million. This phenomenon can be traced back to aggressive land speculation and investment in property, especially in the south and central part of the state. Florida took advantage of this economic boom and its image as a tropical paradise and began to attract more and more investors. Optimistic land developers purchased big tracts of land, built basic infrastructure, divided up the land and speculated using land parcels. Thanks to the newly built railroads, the earnings outlook was good and

tourists have disappeared. The airplane has brought many visitors directly to these attractions – and not just Americans any more, rather tourists from all over the world. These mega theme parks now also offer visitors hotels on site where they can stay. This has isolated visitors from the rest of Florida and has created a monopoly. Also, the impact of millions of visitors on the environment has been ignored for decades. Even Miami has had to make an effort to attract more visitors. In the 1990's, however, the city reinvented itself and – supported by TV shows like Miami Vice, cheap flights and the cruise industry as well as tourists and investors from Latin America – boosted its power of attraction.

In 2000, the tourist industry in Florida created 663,000 jobs and 70 million visitors spent $550 billion dollars in the state.

construction projects were completed at a breath-taking speed. Land speculators made a fortune. New communities popped up, ambitious development projects were completed. Miami became a metropolis. Carl G. Fisher built the new vacation resort Miami Beach.[57] However, by 1925, the market was saturated and the high prices were no longer sustainable. Then, a series of hurricanes hit the state hard, damaging many cities and utilities, thus bringing the real estate prices down with them. In August of 1929, the United States fell into a recession followed by the stock market crash in October, thus officially ending the economic boom and signaling the start of the Great Depression. A decade of high unemployment, poverty, profit losses, deflation and negative economic growth followed. Florida's economy had already been weakened by the land boom. As part of the "New Deal," (1933-40) the government invested heavily in Florida, creating thousands of new jobs and saving the state from major economic damage. In view of the impending world war, the military selected Florida as its main training support base: the Navy went to the coast and the Army went inland. Florida's economy recovered in the wake of war preparations.

The aftermath of the Second World War created renewed prosperity in America with many families entering the middle class and living the American dream, which included house, car and vacation. For many, the dream of visiting or moving to Florida was in reach. For all these reasons, the

Florida's population doubled in the 1950's from 2.7 million to 5 million.

Prosperity and increased life expectancy made the seasonal pilgrimage to Florida a new kind of phenomenon. Middle class families from the north spent the winter in Florida, where they purchased second homes. In 2003, almost a million people owned a second home in Florida.

The second wave of immigration flooded in from the Caribbean. It began in 1959 with the Cuban Revolution followed by other Caribbean islands as well as Central and South America. The Hispanic and Latin population added spice to the culture and society of South Florida. Florida's population today is far more multicultural than its southern neighbors, and since the1960's, has also enjoyed greater prosperity, diversity and urbanity. Its close proximity to Cuba and the Caribbean as well as Central and South America have made Florida the multicultural society that it is today.

The high-tech boom in the early 1990's hit Florida hard: 200,000 jobs were lost in just 18 months. The value of new homes fell by 14 % in 1991 and by an additional 4.3 % in 1992. Eastern Airlines and Pan American Airlines – the latter being the largest airline in the world which controlled almost all international air traffic – went bankrupt. Both airlines got their start in Florida. Once again there were empty building and homes. However, there were also millionaires who sought refuge in Florida and who were welcomed, along with their millions. Hurricane Andrew and the destruction

O'ER THE RAMPARTS WE WATCH

UNITED STATES
ARMY AIR FORCES

it left in its wake created an enormous wave of investment resulting from the insurance claims and government aid. By 2000, Florida was back in business with a million vacation homes and apartments.

Prosperity returned – but this time on an even larger scale. New wealth created new forms of luxury, which, in turn, attracted more affluent people and the nouveau riche. Gated communities with private landing strips and security services where the wealthy can live isolated from the rest of the world have grown in number. Within a decade, real estate prices shot through the roof, with luxury homes being built that were not only more expensive, but grew larger and larger. The number of golf courses multiplied and consumed immense quantities of water from an already heavily compromised eco-system.

Between 2001 and 2006, home and property values in larger cities, such as Tampa and Miami, grew by more than 80 percent to never-before-seen prices. This so-called real estate bubble burst between 2007 and 2008, kicking off the global financial crisis – seen by many as the worst economic crisis since the Great Depression – and taking a big bite out of Florida's economy.

The Defense Industry

■ The Consequences
of the Second World War

Although the Second World War took place far from the shores of the US, Florida was heavily impacted by it. After it was selected

Cape Canaveral Air Force Station, north of Cocoa Beach

as the main support base for the U.S. Army and Navy, the military presence in Florida became massive. Numerous military bases were built and recruits from all over the country came to Florida for boot camp and training. The United States Army Air Forces (USAF) built many air bases for submarine defense and for pilot training in USAAF fighter jets and bombers. These bases included the Jacksonville Naval Air Station, the Mayport Naval Station, Cecil Field Naval Air Station, Whiting Field Naval Air Station and Homestead Air Force Base. Most air force bases were under the command of the Third Air Force or the Army Air Forces Training Command (AAFTC). Some of the bases, however, were controlled by base commands, such as Air Technical Service Command (ATSC) and Air Transport Command (ATC) or the Troop Carrier Command. At the end of the war, Florida was home to 175 military installations.[58] The communities surrounding these bases were fearful that they would close when the war ended. Some of the installations were, in fact, used for other purposes. The Hendricks Army Airfield – combat training base B-17 Flying Fortress – was transformed into the Sebring's Regional Airport.[59] Another section

of it was turned into the Sebring International Raceway,[60] where racecars have been racing since 1950. Marianna Army Field was transformed into a state tuberculosis hospital. The Carlstrom Field in Arcadia was also turned into a hospital. The Dale Mabry Army Air Field barracks was turned into a student dormitory for the local branch of the University of Florida in Tallahassee. The unexpected rise in student numbers resulting from the "GI Bill," which entitled veterans to receive government grants for further education, led to many colleges being founded on former military airfields and bases.[61] In December 1945, only 70 of the original 175 military installations were under the military's control.[62]

■ The Cold War and the Space Race

In 1948, the Cold War had just begun when Cape Canaveral was founded at the Banana River Naval Air Station in Brevard County as a testing base for long-range rockets. The site was selected due to its favorable geographical location and the already existing military bases in Florida. It is now known as Patrick Air Force Base. In 1951, the Air Force also built the Air Force Missile Test Center. The first rocket launched on July 24, 1950 from Cape Canaveral was a RTV-G-4 bumper, a combination of German V-2 rockets and a sounding rocket (WAC-Corporal). After successful flights like Viking 11(1954) and 12 (1955) from White Sands in southern New Mexico, sub-orbital rocket flights were then launched from Cape Canaveral in 1956.

NASA (National Aeronautics and Space Administration) was founded in 1958 with a clear civilian, non-military orientation. It was intended to support the peaceful use of technology in space research and combined broad fields of technology and research in one agency.

During the Second World War, the Naval Air Station in Pensacola had become the world's largest Marine Fighter Air Base. With the replacement of propeller planes by jet planes, 6000 pilots completed their training over a period of three years in Pensacola during the Korean War.[63] The Eglin Air Force Base along with the Air Proving Ground Center was renamed the Armament Development and Test Center in 1968. It bundles research, development and testing of non-nuclear munitions for the air force. In 1989, the Center was responsible for producing precision laser, TV or infrared-controlled weapons, two tank defense weapon systems and an improved weapon for stationary targets (GBU-28), all of which were used in Operation Desert Storm during the First Gulf War.[64]

Orlando, too, underwent changes as a result of the Korean War. The Orlando Air Force Base (AFB)[65] was re-opened in 1951 as a training facility for air and space engineers. The air force additionally re-acquired the former Pinecastle Army Airfield which was used for air training command and later handed over to strategic air command. Through this massive military expansion program (MILCON), the airfield was changed into a training base for the new B-47 Stratojet medium bomber aircraft. In the 1950's and 60's, the Orlando Air Force Base became the central location for numerous air force units and training facilities until it was put under the Navy's control in 1967. The Orlando Air Force Base became the Orlando Naval Training

Center (NTC Orlando) for more than 5,000 Navy recruits. The training equipment, including flight simulators, was moved to NTC Orlando. The Naval Nuclear Power Training Command (NNPTC) was founded for training all personnel in the Navy's nuclear power program. In the 1970's and 80's, the NTC Orlando was a vast complex that contributed $575 million annually to Central Florida's economy. In 1991, $1.8 billion from the defense industry flowed into the city of Orlando's coffers, followed by $1.4 billion going to Jacksonville. Another important defense industry center is Tampa. The MacDill Air Force Base[66] was selected as the headquarters for special deployment command and, from there, controlled various deployments for the Army, Air Force, Navy and Marine Corps. The Avon Park Air Force Range[67] under the command of the MacDill AFB is additionally an important training ground for air force pilots.

Florida as Senior Citizen Paradise

Ponce de León once came to Florida to search for the fountain of youth. Since then, Florida has always been associated with

the idea of eternal youth. Sun, sea and sand attract millions of young students to Florida each year for spring break – a tradition that began back in the 1950's. The state is also known as a stronghold for plastic surgery and the anti-aging industry. In addition to its power to draw millions of young people to its shores each year, Florida's mild climate is also a magnet for millions of senior citizens and retirees. During the 20th century, a unique demographic change took place in that the Babyboomer generation began to get older. Between 1900 and 2000, life expectancy rose by more than 30 years, which meant that retirees had time and money on their hands. The concept of aging had to be redefined which Florida

Skyline of Miami

succeeded in doing by offering active senior citizen communities accompanied by assisted living when needed.

The demographic change was also visible in the political arena. Despite the support of many seniors for the Democrats, the Republican party experienced a rebirth there.

A New Lifestyle

The cities of Florida were traditionally less densely populated compared to other American cities and expanded horizontally with smaller city centers. However, starting in 1950, its cities grew into metropolises with the highest growth rates in the USA. Where there were once small towns and rural communities, suburban housing developments and densely populated retirement communities now grew.

Miami is now a 21st century metropolis and one of the most important cities worldwide. Its influence is noticeable and has spread beyond northern and southern borders. It is a city of contradictions, where poverty and luxury live side by side. Miami's influence is global. Orlando's influence, on the other hand, is mainly statewide. The city's economy and number of residents had already expanded prior to the opening of Disney World, but with its opening in 1971, it experienced an unprecedented change so fundamental that it gave the city completely new identity. The impact of 40 million tourists annually on the city was enormous.

Planning and growth regulations in Florida were almost unknown at that time, resulting in access roads being overloaded and major problems with wastewater disposal. Gigantic freeways were built in this way that had a negative impact on downtown areas and destroyed much fertile farmland. Aside from these problems, such urban development enabled the working class to be able to afford to buy homes. Floridians prefer single-family homes in suburban areas which means they are dependent on their cars. However, in the 1980's and 1990's, downtown areas began to revive economically, thus fighting this flight to suburbia.

Politicians heavily promoted the downtown revival by attracting investors. Moreover, a booming economy, financially strong companies and monetary donations contributed to a cultural renaissance in many of Florida's towns and cities. In a wave of private and publicly funded construction projects between 1980 and 2000, new libraries, colleges, museums, theaters and art galleries were built. The Florida Bureau of Historic Preservation was founded in 1983. This organization identified the historical significance of many buildings and awakened a new awareness for the character of the city and for appreciating the past.

The Most Recent Trends

For the USA and for Florida, the 21st century has brought with it unimaginable events that have shaken the positive image of the Sunshine State over the long term. The first of these events was the Presidential election of the year 2000 during which Florida become the main stage of a nationwide controversy: The number of votes cast for candidates Al Gore (Democrats) and George W. Bush (Republicans) was very close and an automatic recount became necessary. The recounts triggered a huge controversy throughout the country. Complaints about vote manipulation, voter fraud and heavy criticism against the diverse voting systems became loud and was accompanied by the 36-day volley of controversial court decisions at all levels. In the end, the Supreme Court had to intervene to stop the ongoing recounts that the Florida Supreme Court had ordered and declared that Bush had won the election with a majority 0.009 percent more votes than Gore. The election debacle of 2000 reawakened old political tensions within society and reignited the call for election reform in Florida.

Florida's ecosystems paid a heavy price for growth and development. The deterioration of the Everglades went hand in hand with the considerable changes that the development of Florida's once beautiful and unique landscape caused. The coastline was changed, canals, lagoons and rivers newly created or dramatically changed. These interventions, driven by rising real estate prices, had a considerable environmental impact. Many wildlife species, such as the Florida panther, the manatee and the Key deer almost went extinct. Since 2000, the once impenetrable and optimistic dream of progress in Florida has been shaken again and again by natural catastrophes such as hurricanes, freezes, forest fires and droughts. The American Dream there has turned out to be unsustainable.

The ecosystem is in danger. Maintaining balance has cost tax payers billions of dollars. Rescuing the Everglades was an expensive undertaking and the results anything but satisfactory – despite the $8 billion that were made available for the restoration of the Everglades.

Environmental pollution caused by high population densities, garbage and wastewater disposal, agriculture and CO_2 emissions are and remain the main challenges facing Florida today. A great deal of political will is needed to protect Florida's water, air and land and to stop the decline of coral reefs and animal species as well as protecting the entire Everglades ecosystem.

Florida is traditionally a region that is a magnet for powerful storms and hurricanes. However, due to the high density population in coastal areas, the storms that powered through the state in the 2000's caused immense property damage and almost led to the ruin of the insurance industry. Where there were once coastal wetlands and waterways that partially blocked the path of such storms and lessened their force, now these are heavily populated residential areas. Vacation resorts and homes were built anywhere that had a view of the ocean. Without buffer land, which cushions the capricious changes in the coastline caused by nature, the erosion of beaches has led to an expensive problem. On the other hand, the damages caused by such storms are followed by reconstruction and government aid, which, in turn, keeps the construction industry in business. In view of global warming and climate change, Florida may be facing even more powerful storms in the future. Throughout its history, the state has seen a multitude of changes. However, it has always understood how and succeeded in redefining itself in order to adapt to new circumstances and challenges. Today, Florida is one of the most modern US states with Miami as its flagship city and economic powerhouse. Time will tell how Florida handles the challenges of the 21st century and whether it will be successful in mastering them.

Isabel Brücher

USEFUL INFORMATION ON FLYING IN FLORIDA

■ Climate

Florida has a subtropical climate, which is why it attracts many Americans from the north, in particular, during the winter. It also enjoys great popularity among Europeans. Even if there are considerable temperature fluctuations between north Florida and Key West, for example, there are at least 3 relatively uniform seasons. From June to September, the weather there is hot and humid with many thunder storms as well as hurricanes. During this period, flight conditions are more difficult to calculate which is why summer in Florida is not the best time to travel there.

The seasonal transitions from October to November and March to May are better times to travel to Florida. These months enjoy mainly summer-like temperatures without much precipitation. However, the closer you get to the high summer season, the weather becomes a more critical factor, because conditions can arise that make VFR flights impossible. So don't plan your trip too close to the summer months.

Winter is the best time for flying in Flo-

■ Climate Table for Jacksonville in °C

Month	JAN	FEB	MAR	APR	MAY	JUN	JUL	AUG	SEPT	OCT	NOV	DEC	YEAR
Daytime temperature	18	20	23	27	30	32	33	33	31	27	23	19	26.3
Nighttime temperature	6	7	10	14	18	21	23	23	20	15	10	7	14.5
Hours of sun / day	6	7	8	9	10	8	8	8	6	7	6	6	7.3
Days of rain	7	7	7	6	7	11	13	12	14	11	6	7	108
Water temperature	17	17	18	20	23	26	29	30	29	27	24	20	23

rida because the weather conditions are more stable. From December to March, evenings can become cold quickly, leaving frost on the plane's surfaces by early morning. However, it disappears quickly if the plane is left outside in the open because the day-time temperatures rise again quickly to around 20°C / 68°F. Pilots prefer to fly in the winter because the weather is generally good for VFR flying and it is usually easy to predict.

■ Licenses

To fly N-registered airplanes, you have to have an FAA license that was either validated, converted or obtained normally as an independent license in the USA.

For foreigners, the easiest way to obtain an FAA license is to have your own license validated. Most flight schools can help you with the preliminary steps. The process itself essentially consists of informing the FAA which licenses you have and which you want validated. Secondly, you have to allow the issuing authority to pass this information on to the FAA or confirm it. To do so, you only have to submit one form, that is easy to fill in and should be sent to the FAA headquarters 2-3 months prior to travel. Due to government budget cuts, staff at the FAA has been considerably reduced which, to some extent, has resulted in substantial delays in getting licenses issued and validated. That's why it's important to get your paperwork in as early as possible.

■ Climate Table for Miami in °C

Month	JAN	FEB	MAR	APR	MAY	JUN	JUL	AUG	SEPT	OCT	NOV	DEC	YEAR
Daytime temperature	24	25	26	28	30	31	33	33	33	30	27	25	28.6
Nighttime temperature	15	15	18	19	22	23	25	25	24	22	19	16	20.2
Hours of sun / day	7	8	9	10	10	10	10	9	9	9	8	7	8.8
Days of rain	5	6	6	6	9	10	13	16	14	11	7	5	108
Water temperature	22	22	23	25	27	29	30	31	30	28	26	24	26

Directly after arriving in Florida, the flight school will schedule an appointment with the local FSDO (Flight Standards District Office) that you must personally attend. The friendly employees on site will chat with you for a while to find out whether your English is good enough to handle American radio communication. But don't worry! This is not a language test and you will not be graded, but the FAA does want to ensure that everyone on radio communication channels has basic English language skills. Most people usually come out of this appointment with a "Temporary Airman Certificate," which allows you to fly in the USA. After about 3 months, you should receive the compact FAA license in the mail, which is the size of a credit card. This license is valid indefinitely as long as no changes are made to your underlying license. Also, all restrictions from your original license apply to this one. For example, if your European license does not include a night rating, you will not be allowed to fly at night in the USA, even though a normal American license includes a night rating. If these rules aren't already complicated enough for a PPL SEP Land license, then it gets more complicated for more advanced licenses. Once you have your "Temporary Airman Certificate," theoretically, you are authorized to fly. But before you can hire a charter plane, you have to undergo checkout through the flight school. More

on this further on in the book.

Those who want to convert their licenses should obtain detailed information in advance on the individual requirements, which are different depending on the license - PPL or CPL, VFR or IFR. What they all have in common is the fact that you have to re-take exams that will pave the way toward obtaining a stand-alone FAA license.

For those who have obtained their license in the USA according to FAA regulations, and who have passed a valid medical exam and a current biennial flight review can skip all aforementioned procedures and start directly with checkout.

This checkout generally consists of about one hour of ground school to become familiar with the unique nature of American air space and then one hour in the air. Make sure that at the end of checkout, you record somewhere in writing that you have gone through the process – the best place is your logbook. In case of an accident, the insurance company will want to know that you have undergone proper checkout instruction. Also, ask about which plane models you are currently checked out for. There are some schools where checkout in a C172R does not necessarily authorize you to also fly a C172SP, even if both have the same instrumentation.

It is also entirely possible to have a more

in-depth checkout process so that it can also be simultaneously entered as a biennial flight review (BFR) into your logbook.

■ Flight Preparation

We hope that this book gives you many reasons to fly to new and different locations so you can experience the freedom and beauty of Florida from the air. What makes the Sunshine State stand out is its broad range of daytrip destinations – from pure sightseeing flights over incredible landscapes to special destinations for golfers, natural scientists, ornithologists, beach lovers, and more. The FAA no longer requires hardcopy maps in the cockpit so that the usual line on the sectional is no longer necessary. Nevertheless, you should think about where you want to fly beforehand because there are some flight restrictions, even in the USA. So, it's still a good idea to have the old-fashioned chart available as a good basis for planning. For those who prefer to plan online, try this portal: www.skyvector.com. Here, you can enter routes and use Drag&Drop lines to bypass areas that you want to avoid. Another outstanding planning tool is the iPad app called Foreflight. This app offers all current sectionals, airport data as well as frequencies. With an Internet connection, current weather data and, if applicable, temporary flight restrictions (TFRs) can also be displayed. All air spaces are displayed and whoever has an iPad with a GPS also has a complete moving map in the cockpit. It quickly provides an overview of where you are. And anyone who isn't sure what air space they are in or which air space the difficult-to-see light blue line highlights can press on the questionable area for 1-2 seconds and precise information on the air space class, including upper and lower limit, will appear. An especially helpful feature has proven to be the automatic generation of waypoints into traffic pattern and can be found under the "Procedures" button. Here, you can decide whether you want to fly straight in or enter the pattern at a 45-degree angle to the airport. Those who want to try out the app before purchasing it, can do so for thirty days free of charge. For most pilots, this trial period should be long enough for a flying holiday.

Those traveling without a tablet and with an FAA license can register with www.duat.com and receive all necessary information, especially NOTAMs and weather conditions for the entire route. Furthermore, there is a cost-free and outstanding telephone service called WX BRIEF, which is especially useful for NOTAMs and weather information. By dialing the 1-800 WX BRIEF at no charge, you receive all the information you need for flight planning from a single source. When doing so, you should put some thought into your flight beforehand, including the duration of the flight and altitude as well as the type of airplane. You then give this information to the briefer in advance so that he can customize his briefing accordingly. Some briefers appreciate receiving all the information on the scheduled flight at one time. A call with WX BRIEF would then go something like this: You dial 1800WXBRIEF or 1-800-992-7433. An automated service answers first, it asks you to select the region that you would like a briefing for and you are then forwarded to the appropriate team. As soon as someone answers, which usually takes 30 seconds or less, you would make your request by saying something like this:

"Good morning, my name is Udo, I am planning a VFR flight from KABC to KXYZ in a C172, estimated time en route 50 minutes at 4500 ft, estimated time of departure 0900 LT (or give Zulu time). The callsign is N-AV8R. I would like a full briefing."

Your briefer will then give you all weather information and NOTAMs at the departure and destination airports as well as along the route. He will also give you information about the winds aloft for your flight.

Briefers do not normally give recommendations as to whether a flight can be made or not based on weather, unless you are planning an VFR flight and the airport reports IFR. The person on the other end of the line is not a qualified meteorologist who can give you a personal forecast, rather the briefer gives you only the terminal area forecast (TAF). The information is standardized in its format and briefers do not like to be interrupted nor do they like to deviate from the standards. In other words, if you request a full briefing, you will also receive one even if you also already know the weather conditions at your departure airport. There is also a shortened briefing format. However, I recommend always requesting the full format because it is easy to oversee something when doing your own planning. A few additional minutes on the phone with the briefer is time well-invested.

Then there is also the Flight Watch Service, an outstanding cost-free service nationwide, which is available everywhere at an altitude of at least 5000 ft at 122.0 and from where pilots can request or submit current weather information (pilot reports). Each region has its own Flight Watch Center which is responsible for their respective sector. If however you do not know which regional center is currently responsible for you, you are allowed to drop the regional name from the callsign and simply call "Flight Watch"

instead of "Miami Flight Watch:"
"Flight Watch, this is N-AV8R VFR from KABC to KXYZ, 10nm south of XXX VOR at 6000 ft. I would like to have the latest weather information en route and at KXYZ."

■ Flight Performance

Your checkout with a flight instructor will definitely give you an idea of the differences between flying in the US and in your own country. Those used to flying with an approach map on hand will definitely be pleased about how much more freedom to fly there is in the USA. Though the usual regulations on noise abatement apply in this country, there are generally no strict instructions on how to approach the airfield, except for the direction of the traffic pattern (left as a rule). However, to demonstrate good airmanship, you should fly the traffic pattern so that you can land at any time on the runway in case of an engine failure. Here, the pilot has greater personal obligations – which is also the case in other areas of flying. For example, it is completely normal for the info frequency (CTAF or Unicom) to not always be listened to at uncontrolled air fields. Nevertheless, you can land at any time even if no one on the ground is responding. That makes it all the more important to listen to the radio

from the cockpit and to regularly give reports to inform others of your own plan in the airfield or during your approach and to coordinate with them.

■ VFR Flight Following

In the USA you can also fly VFR without talking to anyone. Legally, this is no problem, at least in uncontrolled air space. In principle, you basically make do without the 2nd set of eyes that watch you in the air - also in the blind spots directly below or above your plane, when entering a new waypoint into your GPS or looking for the next frequency on the sectional. But is that still good airmanship?
What exactly is VFR Flight Following? VFR Flight Following is a radar service that is offered by the Terminal Radar Approach Control (TRACON) or Air Route Traffic Control Centers (ARTCC). Using a squawk code, the airplane is identified on the controller's radar screen, provided it is equipped with a transponder. If the controller identifies the airplane, he can give the pilot traffic information or issue warnings. This means that for flights at lower altitudes, warnings regarding obstacles or terrain are issued. Should you need vectors to get around these obstacles, you have to request them. Controllers themselves will only give you vectors in order to separate you from IFR traffic.

Furthermore, controllers have at their disposal real-time information that can help them to keep your flight route as short as possible. This affects both the status of restricted areas as well as military operation areas (MOAs) that you are legally allowed to fly through, but ATC knows whether the MOA is currently "hot" or not. Flying through class C might also be an option for a shortcut. You don't even need a clearance to enter it, but you have to have established 2-way radio communications with the corresponding approach frequency. In concrete terms, 2-way radio communications is established when ATC has read back your callsign.
- "N-AV8R, stand by!" is sufficient in this case. You may fly into class C air space, clearance is not issued.
But you can also fly into air space B as long as the controller has given you the necessary clearance. In this case, explicit clearance is required.

"N-AV8R, you are cleared into the Bravo at or below 3000 ft."

Just as important as flight route optimization is that you are already in radio contact with someone who can help you if you have an emergency situation. If there is an emergency, it may otherwise be hours before a rescue can be organized. Even with an activated flight plan, initial search activities do not begin until at least 30 minutes after the ETA.

Even if safety under Flight Following rises considerably, there are two issues you can't lose sight of:

1. VFR Flight Following is an extra task for the controller whose main task is to separate IFR traffic. This means that, under certain circumstances, a busy controller may not answer your first call or find time to provide you with additional information although he has you on the radar with Squawk Code. The same also applies to handovers to other frequencies if you leave a sector. If he has no time to hand you over to the next sector, he simply terminates the service; maybe giving you the frequency for the next sector, but then you have to re/state your intentions.

2. Remember that you are always the Pilot in Control. The pilot always has the last say! Should you choose not to follow the controller's instructions, e.g. to remain in VMC, you are obligated to inform him of this immediately.

■ Phraseologe
Yhe person on the other end of the line is always a very busy professional. So make sure you behave just as professionally. Think about what you want to say and keep it short. Always listen to the frequency for a few minutes to get

a feeling of what's going on in the ATC. If you get an instruction that you didn't understand, ask. It may be embarrassing and you may get an annoyed response from the controller, but it even happens to professionals and it is always better to be safe than sorry when flying in controlled airspace.

Here are a few examples:

Establishing contact

- JAX Approach, this is N-AV8R, with request.
- N-AV8R, Jax Approach, state your request.
- N-AV8R, a PA28, just departed St. A ugustine, 1500 feet climbing 4500, request VFR flight following into Lake City.
- N-V8R squawk 0815 and ident.
- Squawk 0815, N-V8R.
- N-V8R, radar contact established, 10 nm northwest of St. Augustine. You have traffic at 2 o' clock, 2nm, a Cessna 172 flying southbound.
- Traffic in sight, maintain visual separation, N-V8R.
Or
- Negative traffic, N-V8R.

Handover to next station

- N-V8R, contact Tallahassee Approach on 135.8.
- Contact Tallahassee Approach on 135.8, N-V8R.

- Tallahassee Approach, N-AV8R, now with you at 4500 ft.
- N-AV8R, Tallahassee altimeter is 3001.
- Altimeter is 3001, N-AV8R.

Approach to destination airport

- N-V8R, report Lake City in sight.
- N-V8R has Lake City in sight.
- N-AV8R, Jax Approach, radar service terminated, squawk 1200.
- Squawk VFR, N-AV8R.

This list of examples is in no way complete. It is meant to just give you an initial idea. If you want a better idea of how radio traffic in the USA works, try listening to different frequencies at www.liveatc.net. However, don't start right off with JFK in New York – and get intimidated – it's much better to start with a smaller, local airport like St. Augustine or Boca Raton. After listening a few times, you will find that you get used to the fast-talking controllers.

NORTH

FLORIDA

- ■ Apalachicola Regional Airport
- ■ Cedar Key - George T Lewis Airport
- ■ Gainesville
- ■ Jekyll Island, GA
- ■ Lake City Gateway Airport
- ■ Quincy
- ■ St. Augustine -
Northeast Florida Regional Airport
- ■ St. Simons - Malcolm McKinnon Airport, GA
- ■ Tallahassee Regional Airport
- ■ Williston Municipal Airport

KAAF

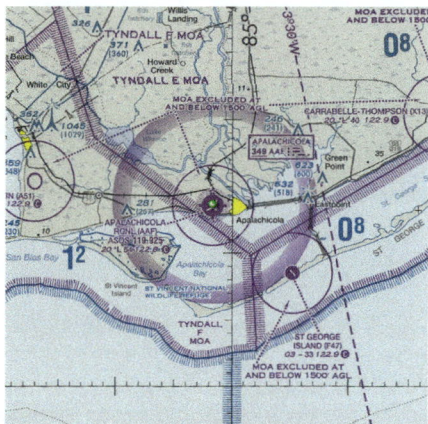

APALACHICOLA REGIONAL AIRPORT

R W Y
14-32 5425 x 150 ft.
2-light PAPI, left

06-24 5271 x 150 ft.
2-light PAPI, left

18-36 5251 x 150 ft.

CTAF/UNICOM: 122.8
ASOS: 119.925
(☎ 850-653-8271)

SERVICE

JET A, 100LL
Crooms Taxi Service
☎ 850-653-8132,
Courtesy car 4-5 Pers.
Very helpful FBO

Those who visit Apalachicola today may have a hard time imagining that this quaint fishing village used to be the third most important port in the Gulf of Mexico. At that time, sponge diving, driven by the Greek immigrants who settled there, was the port's economic engine. Nowadays, its most important product is oysters. Almost all of Florida's oyster production takes place in the Apalachicola bay. Protected by the offshore islands St. Vincent and St. George, the breeding conditions for oysters are perfect.

Apalachicola is a nice small American town. There are still mom and pop stores, restaurants, cafés, and ice cream parlors and no shopping mall for as far as the eye can see. Of course, eating oysters here goes without saying. Though unlike Europe, they are not served raw, but are usually roasted or fried. If you want your oysters raw, you have to order them that way especially.

The approach to Apalachicola is definitely one of the most scenic in North Florida. The Apalachicola River forms a wildly extensive river delta that flows out into the ocean, and from the cockpit, it is the perfect landmark. Those who want an extended approach can also fly over the offshore islands. If you choose this approach, then make sure you check the traffic around St. George airfield. Prior to flying in, it is highly recommended that

you contact Tyndall Approach (124.15 or 125.2) for traffic information. If the MOA is active, you can then expect intense military flight traffic.

The Apalachicola airport with its cross runways is convenient to fly into, the FBO is small but very helpful. The airport courtesy car gets you into town in just a few minutes for a bite to eat and a walk through town.

The Grady Market

LINK

www.apalachicolabay.org

Its many brick buildings give the downtown a distinct character.

53

KCDK

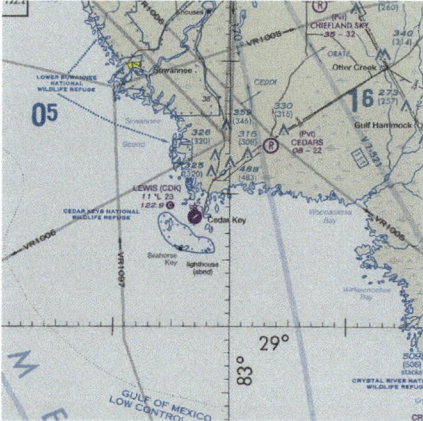

R W Y	05-23 • 2355 x 100 ft.

| (•) | CTAF 122.9 |

SERVICE

No fuel station.
Taxi: 352-949-2127
Golf Cart: 352-543-5090

Enjoy a meal right on the water

CEDAR KEY - GEORGE T LEWIS AIRPORT

Cedar Key is a small offshore island between Waccasassa Bay and the Suwannee Sound and is located in the northernmost part of the Gulf of Mexico. Even just the approach over Waccasassa Bay or Withlacoochee Bay is very exciting. Flying from the mainland, you can see how farmland turns into swamp and marshland, the water slowly gains the upper hand until you are finally flying over the ocean. It's a quick flight because Cedar Key is just barely offshore, so don't bother packing your life vests.

There isn't much going on here during the week, but weekends are very busy because the island is popular among the locals for swimming, fishing, boating or a quick ride on their Harley. The small airport is operated with American pragmatism, which might take some getting used to for Europeans. The taxiway can be a bit chaotic at peak arrival times with airplanes, cars, pedestrians and bicyclists everywhere, but somehow it all works out. Like I said, pragmatism is the law of the land here. You can park on both sides of the taxiway. What is also unusual is that upon your approach you are asked over the CTAF frequency whether you need a shuttle into town. Judy & Gaia operate a very casual taxi service that takes guests to and from Cedar Key for $5 per person. If you are not contacted by radio, you can also call directly (352-949-2127). The taxi will then come directly to your plane.

The beach is small and neat.

LINK
www.gulfkartcompany.com

Colorful wooden buildings line the city streets

Take it easy – in Cedar Key

Alternatively, you can rent the ever-so-popular Florida golf cart from George Oakley. Sometimes, he's just waiting with his carts right at the airport or you can contact him directly. Gulf Kart Company, E-Mail: OakleyG@bellsouth.net, Tel.: 352-543-5090.

With its many colorfully painted wooden buildings, the town exudes a certain southern charm with a touch of hippy. Its best to head first to the pier and then stroll from there toward the town center. If you can do without an ocean view, head toward 2nd Street behind the marina where you will find smaller restaurants that are not as busy. On the same street, there is also a small supermarket where you can buy snacks and groceries for your return flight.

Between the pier and 1st Street is a small marina, where you can rent boats. From there, you can explore your surroundings from the water or you can hire a professional guide to take you out. You should plan 2-3 hours, including food, for a round-trip.

The take-off from runway 23 is notorious: Once in the air, all you see is water and the horizon in front of you, and there are no visible reference points. It's even harder, if you are flying into the sun, or if there is a light haze over the water - then you should concentrate on the instruments and turn toward the left as soon as you have reached a safe altitude. This will put the coastline back into your view.

The small marina is where most pleasure boats are launched from

KGNV

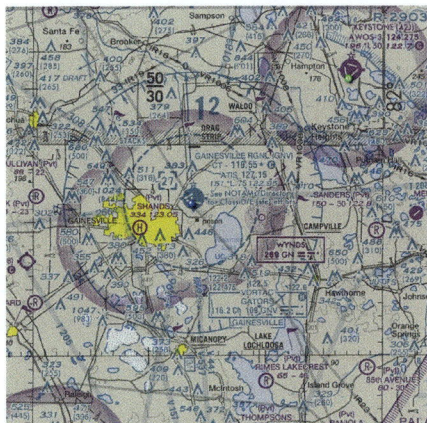

R W Y	11-29 • 7504 x 150 ft.
	11: 4-light PAPI, left
	29: 4-light PAPI, right
	07-25 • 4158 x 100 ft.
	07-25: 4-light PAPI, left

Tower: 119.55
Ground: 121.7
ATIS: 127.15

SERVICE

JET A1, 100LL
University Air Center

Relaxed southern flair

GAINESVILLE

One of the oldest towns in Florida, Gainesville has grown a population of 120,000 - but still carries a relaxed vibe.

The Gainesville airport is no exception. Except for a few regional jets, there's not much going on. Radio contact is no problem – tower frequency is not too busy. And the runway is huge. This relaxed atmosphere is probably one reason why many flight schools in the area send their flight students to Gainesville for their solo cross-country flight.

The University Air Center is very welcoming. Those who fuel up there are given a courtesy car free of charge. Those who want to stay longer can rent a car from AVIS or enterprise. The 10-15 minute drive to town is worth it, because Gainesville has an interesting mix of Victorian and southern architecture. It is also home to the University of Florida, one of the oldest public universities in the United States. In 1995, Gainesville was ranked number 1 by Money Magazine as the city with the highest quality of life. The downtown has several good restaurants. I recommend Harry's for traditional southern dishes and seafood.

LINK

www.uac.aero

Southern style architecture

Street café in Gainesville

The Hippodrome Theatre
in the town center

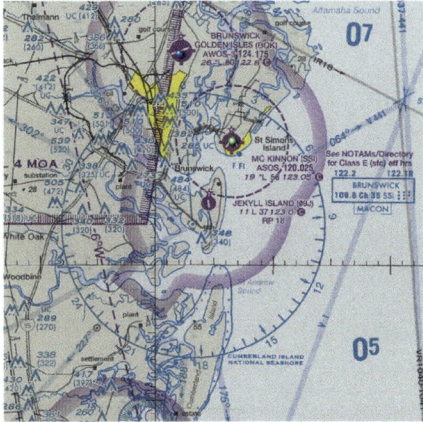

Ø9J

RWY 18-36 · 3715 x 75 ft.
2-light PAPI, left

CTAF/UNICOM: 123.00

SERVICE

No Fuel station.
Electric car rental
Red Bug Motors

Rent a small electric car directly at the airport.

JEKYLL ISLAND

Jekyll Island is a little gem right off the coast of Georgia. Even though it is not a part of Florida, you can reach it quickly from Florida, and it is definitely worth the visit.

When approaching Jekyll Island from the north, be prepared for intense flight traffic north of the island where the Malcolm McKinnon Airport (St. Simons) is located. For noise abatement reasons, airplanes are not allowed to fly over Jekyll Island. That's why the right traffic pattern for runway 18 applies. The airport is infamous for its crosswind which blows in directly from the sea or the land. Furthermore, during landing, look out for a group of trees about 50 ft high at the beginning of runway 18, they can cause wind shears when the wind is coming in from the west. If your aircraft allows, try and touch down behind the treeline to avoid windshear.

Jekyll Island was acquired in 1886 and was used as a wintering ground by the country's wealthiest families at that time. This elite settlement was also dubbed the Jekyll Island Club. Among the 35 founders of the club, which was considered the "richest and most exclusive club in the world," were Joseph Pulitzer and William K. Vanderbilt, to name a few. William Rockefeller and J.P. Morgan joined the club later on. The **Jekyll Island Museum** has saved and restored many items from this era. They are now on display for island visitors. Entrance is free of charge.

The villas —modestly described as "cottages"— that belonged to many club members still adorn the long driveway leading up

The grounds of the Jekyll Island Club –
today a luxury hotel with a beautiful park

to time-honored **Jekyll Island Club Hotel**, one of the most magnificent examples of southern style architecture with its wood and brick design. It has stylishly preserved the brilliance of the past for visitors from the present to enjoy. The hotel, surrounded by a beautiful park setting, dominates the west coast of the island. Today, you can enjoy a meal in the hotel courtyard or a coffee in the local **Starbucks.** The hotel pub does not open until evening.

From the airfield, it's about a 20-30 minute walk to the Jekyll Island Club Hotel and the Jekyll Wharf, which was once used as the hotel dock. At that time, there was no bridge connecting the mainland and the island. The imposing pier is nowadays used as the starting point for **Dolphin Tours** or various fishing tours. As far as restaurants go, you can find **Raw Bar** and **Latitude 31°** directly at the pier. These

Spanish Beard is what the
locals call earth moss.

Sejay's Waterfront Café
at the marina

The old wooden pier is still in good condition

Tying down your airplane here is a must

are two highly recommended restaurants which can get busy very quickly during the high season. If you are able to land a sunny spot directly on the pier, you will enjoy a wonderful view of the Jekyll River. It is an inherent part of the Intracoastal Waterway, though it is not really a river, but more of a strait.

Those lucky enough to spend more time on the island can also rent bicycles from the many bicycle rental companies there. Unfortunately, there is not a bicycle rental station at the airport. If you want to see as much of the island as possible in a short time, then I recommend renting an electric car from **Red Bug Motors**, located right at the airfield. These small, open electric cars enable you to comfortably take a tour of the island and explore its treasures. You can do a nice loop in an hour if you don't make any stops, however, you will miss a lot worth seeing. If you have time, drive the loop and plan to make a few stops along the way, including lunch. You should plan a

*The St. John's River
flows into the sea near Jacksonville*

LINKS

www.jekyllisland.com
www.jekyllclub.com
www.jekyllexperience.com

good 2-3 hours for this. The Wharf and the Club Hotel can get very busy at peak times. To avoid the crowds, you can head south to **Sejay's Waterfront Café**, located right next to the bridge at a small marina.

The east side of the island is covered by endless white sandy beaches – perfect for sun, sand and surf. During my last visit, I saw dolphins swimming just 50 m from the shore. There are also several hotels with various price ranges on the east coast of the island. Almost all of them have direct beach access.

Endless sandy beaches on the east coast of the island

KLCQ

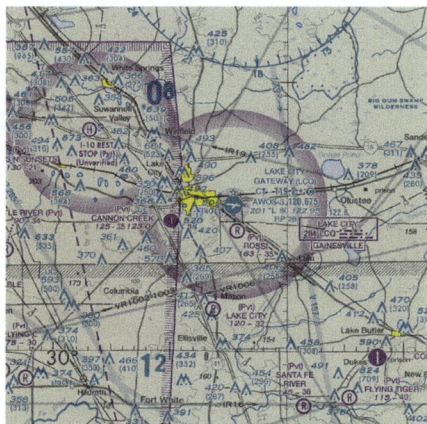

LAKE CITY GATEWAY AIRPORT

Lake City is located almost half way between Jacksonville and Tallahassee. The local airport has a first-class, well-equipped FBO that offers both courtesy cars as well as rental cars (enterprise). Lake City town center is just a 10-minute drive away.

Finding Lake City Airport is not too difficult. Railroad tracks help to give you a good reference point. They run from Jacksonville westward and go right

RWY	
10-28 • 8003 x 150 ft.	*2-light PAPI, left*
05-23 • 4000 x 75 ft.	

CTAF: 119.2
AWOS: 120.675
(☎ 386-754-9366)
Ground: 121.9
Tower: 119.2

SERVICE

JET A1, 100LL
Transport: enterprise, courtesy car

past the airport. The tower frequency is not too busy because flight traffic is on the low side. However, be aware that the tower has relatively early closing times. After 4:30 pm the airport is uncontrolled.

For noise abatement purposes, the right traffic pattern for runway 28 should be used.

It's a long way to Pearl Harbor

Fly yourself around the Bahamas and the wider USA as featured opposite!

www.pilots-paradise.com

- Exclusive PA28 Warrior use for 10 hours (dry).
- Grass strip fly-in home for 2 people
- 2 hours with instructor, who also lives next door, so you are in safe hands
- 1 week

£1395

Please contact us for help gaining an FAA PPL or for any other information

Discover...

Pilots Paradise

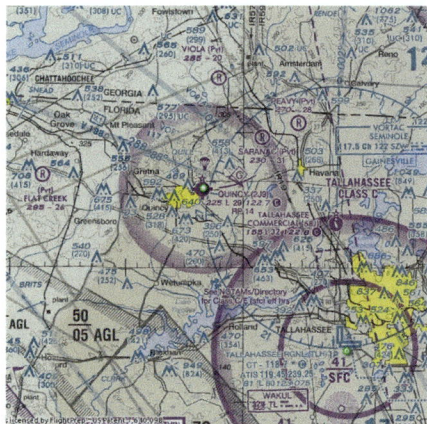

QUINCY

RWY
14-32 • 2964 x 75 ft.
14: 2-light PAPI, right
32: 2-light PAPI, left

CTAF/UNICOM: 122.7

SERVICE

JET A1, 100LL

Quincy is a quieter alternative to the Tallahassee Regional Airport. It's also a very nice place to visit – a small quaint town with southern flair. The Quincy Municipal Airport is located about 1.5 miles from the historic district. There is no FBO at the airport, rather only a very well-managed airport building with basic facilities such as restrooms, beverage and coffee machines. There is a bulletin board in the building where you can find the number for the local taxi service. You can also walk to town – unless you are lucky enough to get a ride with one of the local pilots. After passing many old southern style mansions, you come first to the spiritual center of town, which is characterized by several churches. Keep going until you get to the town center where you will see the colonial style court building. There are several restaurants nearby. Quincy is the capital of Gadsden County which has always been a farming community. The infrastructure here appears older, giving you the impression that Quincy was not gentrified to attract seniors looking for a quiet place to retire. In spite of this or maybe because of this, one of the most famous American woman pilots retired to Quincy: Jerrie Mock, the first woman to fly solo around the world in an airplane. After 29 days, 21 stopovers and about 22,860 miles, she safely landed her Cessna 180 - The Spirit of Columbus - in Columbus, Ohio, on April 17, 1964.

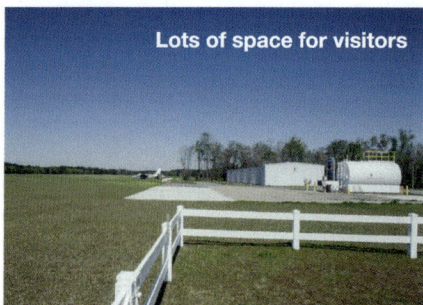

Lots of space for visitors

Court building in Gadsen County

Airport building in Quincy

KSGJ

ST. AUGUSTINE - AIRPORT

St. Augustine is considered the oldest city in North America. It was founded on August 28, 1565 - feast day of St. Augustine - by the Spanish admiral Pedro Menéndez de Avilés. Although there were already other European settlements in Florida, many have been abandoned in the meantime, which now makes St. Augustine the oldest continuously populated city in the United States. The **Castillo de San Marcos** fortress built between 1672 and 1695 located in the center of town was witness to an era during which the Spanish had total control. The fortress and the old town are well preserved and lovingly maintained.

St. Augustine was the capital city of Florida for many years until the capital was moved to Tallahassee in 1824.

Due to its unique historical status, St. Augustine is among the most popular travel destinations in North Florida, especially among Americans. Many Europeans choose St. Augustine as their base for flying holidays because of its excellent tourist infrastructure and its convenient flight connections via the Jacksonville airport. However, if you want to fly here during the peak season, book early, then you will have no problem finding a hotel in any price category. The local flight schools are usually able to help you find the right hotel or lodging and often have discounts at certain locations. It is always worth asking!

Yet St. Augustine has much more to offer than just its history. Miles and miles of sandy beaches are ideal for sunbathing and swimming. At **Alligator Farm** (with

RWY
13-31 • 8002 x 150 ft.
13: 4-box VASI, left
31: 4-light PAPI, left

06-24 • 2701 x 60 ft.
06: 2-light PAPI, left

02-20 • 2610 x 75 ft.

ATIS: 119.625
AWOS: ☎ 904-824-7084
Ground: 121.175
Tower: 127.625

SERVICE

JET A1, 100LL
Rental cars available from enterprise, Hertz

Historic city gate

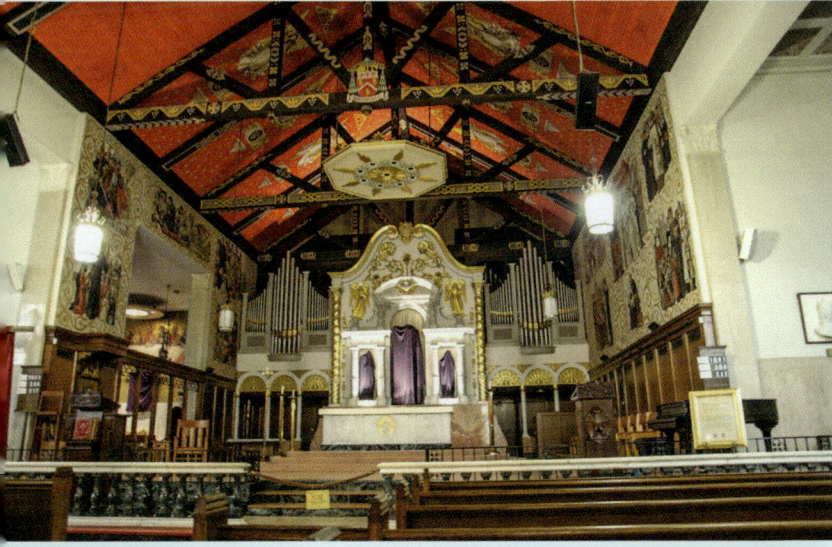

Interior of the basilica from the 18th century

Some of the old houses are lovingly maintained and still lived in

Feeding the alligators

Alligators like to cuddle

Various bird species nest
in the trees

zip line next door), you learn all there is to know about Florida's omnipresent reptiles. The old town also has good pubs and restaurants, offering much more than the usual chain restaurants. Because the St. Augustine airport is at the north end of town, it's a short drive from there to Jacksonville. **Galaxy Aviation** unfortunately does not offer courtesy cars, but it does arrange for rental cars from Hertz. You can get to downtown Jacksonville in about 30/40 minutes from the FBO.

The St. Augustine Airport is a lively place with two large flight schools, many local airplanes and sometimes brisk jet traffic. The main runway runs parallel to the coast which means that you

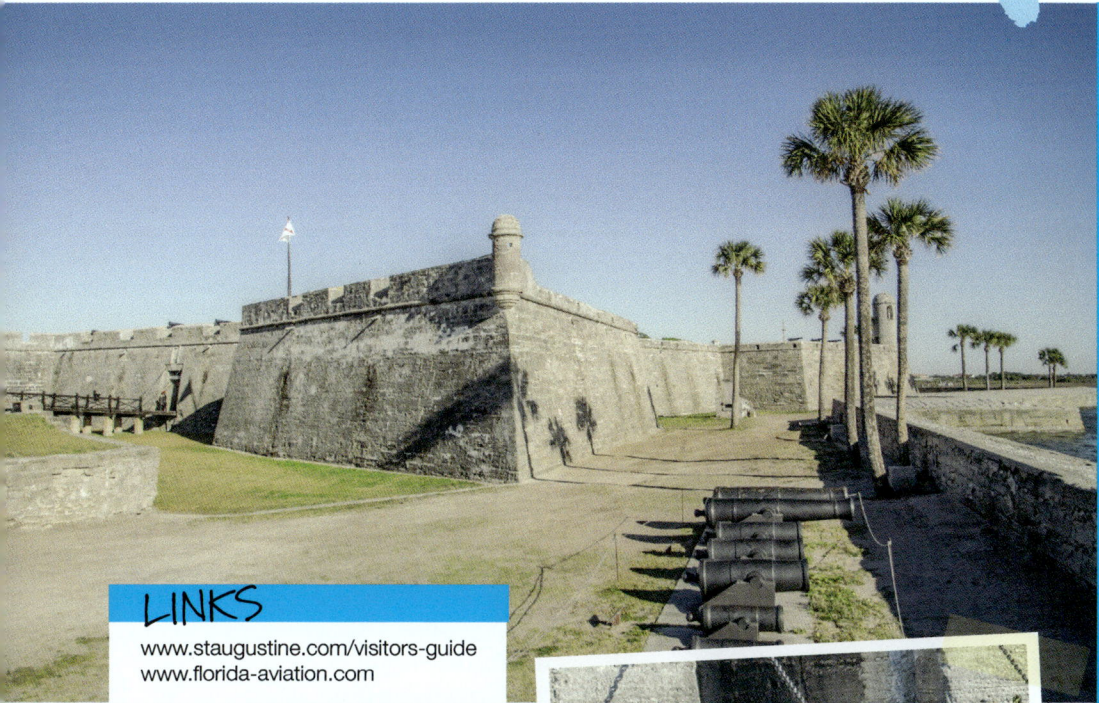

LINKS
www.staugustine.com/visitors-guide
www.florida-aviation.com

often have to deal with a crosswind situation. If air traffic permits, tower tries to accomodate take-offs and landings from the other runways, if requested.

Galaxy is a well-organized FBO that leaves nothing to be desired. If you refuel here, you won't be charged a park-ing fee. The **Fly-by Café** with a slightly raised outdoor patio is located right at the airport (next to the FBO) where you will get a good view of take-offs and landings. With a bit of luck, you may catch some outstand-ing aerobatics training.

A separate aerobatic box has been set up for this purpose. Before enter-ing St. Augustine air space, make sure you listen to the ATIS to find out whether the box is active (hot) or not.

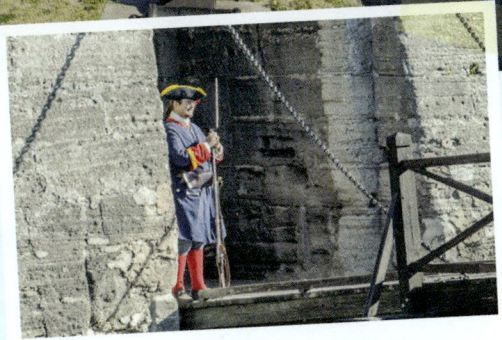

Soldier in period costume – you have to pay an entry fee to go in

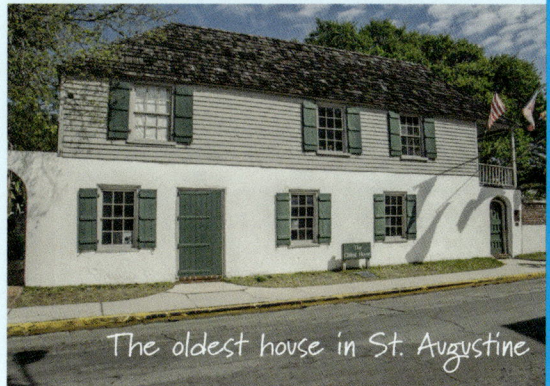

The oldest house in St. Augustine

KSSI

R W Y	04-22 • 5584 x 100 ft. *2-light PAPI, left* 16-34 • 3313 x 75 ft. *2-light PAPI, left*

CTAF/UNICOM: 123.05
ASOS: 120.025 (☎ 912-638-7042)

SERVICE

JET A1, 100LL
Transport: Avis, Hertz, courtesy car

Guests always receive a warm and friendly welcome from the FBO.

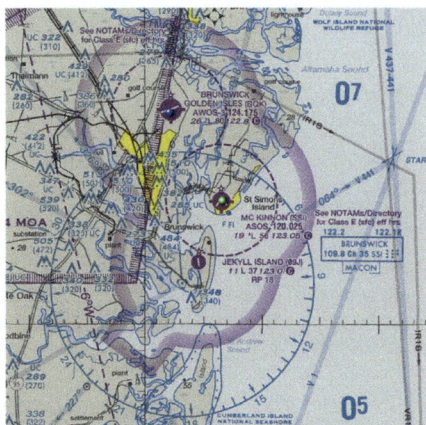

Beautiful island with top BBQ restaurant

ST. SIMONS - MALCOLM MCKINNON AIRPORT

St. Simons is a vacation paradise right off the coast of Georgia. Just 5 nm northeast of the Jekyll Island airfield is the Malcolm McKinnon Airport located on the island of St. Simons. In contrast to Jekyll Island with its short runway, St. Simons has a lot of air traffic, particularly on the weekends. Typical island residents are affluent and this is noticeable everywhere.

There are several different ways to explore St. Simons: One of them is a courtesy car from **Golden Isles Aviation**, the local FBO, or you can head to the bicycle rental shop **Monkeywrench Bicycles** (1708 Frederica Road, Tel 912 634 55), which is about a 10 minute walk. From there, you can comfortably discover the island for yourself. About half way to the bike shop, there is one culinary gem that you just shouldn't miss: **Southern Soul BBQ**. Located in a former gas station, traditional southern dishes are prepared in a rustic atmosphere. Its motto is: "Peace, Love & BBQ". The service is fast and friendly. Try to get a table outside and enjoy the relaxed atmosphere. My favorite dish there is the pulled pork sandwich – I highly recommend it!

If you'd rather play a round of golf, you've come to the right place at **St. Simons Island**. Two of the four courses are open to guests. One course is located right near the airport and can be reached on foot.

The airport itself is uncontrolled. Those who are not used to mixed air traffic with faster planes, have to rethink take-off and landing: A Hawker or a King Air that announce their landing intention when 20 miles away from the landing strip is naturally faster in the traffic pattern than a Cessna 152. You should also keep in mind the potential wake turbulences when business jets take off.

Unconventional and rustic –
Southern Soul BBQ

LINKS

www.explorestsimonsisland.com
www.monkeywrenchbicycles.com

Its motto says it all and the
food is fantastic

73

KTLH

RWY	09-27 • 8003 x 150 ft.
	4-light PAPI, left
	18-36 • 7000 x 150 ft.
	4-light PAPI, left

ATIS: 119.45
ASOS: ☎ 850-576-3665
Ground: 121.9
Tower: 118.7
Tallahassee Approach: 128.7
Tallahassee Departure: 128.7
Clearance Delivery: 126.65

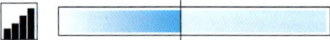

SERVICE

JET A1, 100LL
Transport: Hertz, enterprise,
courtesy cars

The runway length is more than generous

The capital city

TALLAHASSEE REGIONAL AIRPORT

When asked what the capital city of Florida is, most people answer "Miami." Wrong. Tallahassee has been Florida's capital since 1824. Perhaps this confusion is due to Tallahassee being off the beaten track, in the heart of the panhandle or perhaps it's simply because people think it does not have big tourist attractions to offer. Well, nothing could be further from the truth.

Embedded between lakes and national parks, Tallahassee is much more than just a center of government administration. It has a high number of museums, universities and colleges and, with **Embry Riddle Aeronautical University** located there, Tallahassee can boast a recognized training facility for upcoming pilots, aerospace technicians and engineers.

The **Mission San Luis** is Florida's Apalachee-Spanish living museum and brings to life the history of this early European and Native American settlement. The current mission was built on the site where the old Spanish mission was located. Almost all its houses are "inhabited" by people in period costume who transport visitors back in time to show them what life was like during the age of early European settlements. The Mission San Luis is just a 15-minute drive from the airport.

Though the Tallahassee Regional Airport is located in Class C air space, when it comes to air traffic density, it is more

Downtown Tallahassee

like a Class D airport on the east coast. However, you should become familiar with the landing and take-off procedures and, of course, print out your plate and have it on hand. If runway 18-36 is active, the easiest way to get to the FBO is to ask for taxi via "J". This helps you avoid potential zigzagging between the helicopters and business jets. The FBO at this airport, **Million Air**, is one of the top FBOs in Florida. Its services include courtesy and rental cars, quiet rooms, showers and even a pool table.

LINK

www.missionsanluis.org

A model airplane suspended from the ceiling at Million Air

X60

R W Y	05-23 • 6669 x 100 ft. *2-light PAPI, left* 14-32 • 4704 x 100 ft.

CTAF/UNICOM 122.8
AWOS: 118.425 (☎ 352-528-9949)

SERVICE

JET A1, 100LL
City of Williston FBO

Rest stop for travelers

WILLISTON MUNICIPAL AIRPORT

Williston is a quiet place, strategically located about halfway between Gaines-

Rest stop for radial engines

ville and Cedar Key. It is one of those typical airports where pilots land to refuel and/or get something to eat. Right next to the FBO is the Pyper Kub Restaurant which has a nice rustic atmosphere and traditional southern food. The portions are just right and the prices are fair. It's the perfect place for a quick bite before taking off again. Weather permitting, you can sit outside on the patio and watch the action on runway 05-23. The town itself does not have much to offer, so that after refueling and enjoying some good southern cooking, most pilots just head off again.

FLORIDA AVIATION
CAREER TRAINING, INC.

- Part 141 certification since 1991
- flight training for all FAA-airmen certificates
- on-Site Testing for all FAA knowledge exams
- over 2.000 practical exams with 90 % pass rate
- recreational Flying and hour building with or without family
- foreign Licence validation and Conversion
- located in beautiful South European flavored St. Augustine
- living history and 46 miles of Florida´s finest beaches
- accomodations from economy to Five Star
- long term relationship and excellent reputation with the European flying community

www.florida-aviation.com

Tel.: +1 904 824 9401, info@florida-aviation.com

Deutschsprachige Kunden kontaktieren bitte:

Dr. Klaus-Jürgen Schwahn
Tel: +49 170 443 1935, drschwahn@fliegen-usa.de

Spezielle Infos für europäische Flugschüler und Charterkunden:

www.fliegen-usa.de

- Albert Whitted Airport, St. Petersburg
- Chalet Suzanne
- Crystal River
- Deland Municipal Sidney H Taylor Field Airport
- Flagler County Airport
- Inverness Airport
- Kissimmee Gateway Airport
- Lakeland Linder Regional Airport
- Mid Florida Air Service Airport
- New Smyrna Beach Municipal Airport
- Ocala Intl Airport Jim Taylor Field
- Plant City Airport
- River Ranch Resort Airport
- Spruce Creek
- Titusville - Space Coast Regional Airport
- Winter Haven Municipal Airport Gilbert Field
- Zephyrhills Municipal Airport

CENTRAL

FLORIDA

KSPG

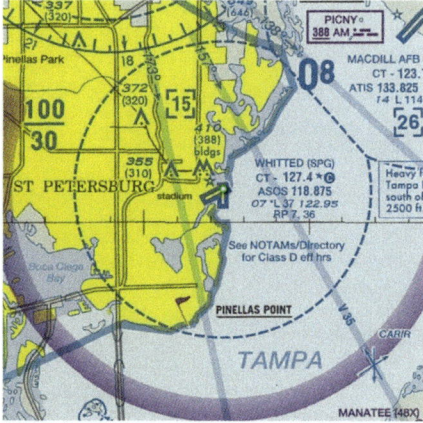

ALBERT WHITTED AIRPORT, ST. PETERSBURG

St. Petersburg has not one, but two founding fathers. The first was John C. Williams, who acquired the land in 1876. The second was Peter Demens, who ensured that the railroad was built as far as St. Petersburg so that the city would be connected to the rest of the state. Demens spent part of his childhood in the Russian city of St. Petersburg which is why he named his new home town St. Petersburg. When the city was officially founded on February 29, 1892, it had 300 inhabitants. Now it has more than 250,000. Over the years, like so many others in the USA, the city has earned several nicknames. One of them is the "Sunshine City" because there are apparently 361 days of sun per year. That's why the city has attracted a certain clientele during the past few decades that has produced another nickname: God's waiting room. In the meantime, however, this demographic imbalance has been rectified. Today, St. Pete - another nickname - has one of Florida's most active art scenes. For example, a good tip for pilots is the **Dalí Museum** located right across from the FBO building. The collection – donated by Reynolds and Eleanor Morse and taking up the ground floor of the museum – has since been added to, making this museum one of the leading Dalí museums in the world.

If you take a left at the museum and head further north, you will come to the marina where you will find **Fresco's Waterfront**

R W Y
07-25 • 3677 x 75 ft.
2-light PAPI, left
18-36 • 2864 x 150 ft.
18: 2-light PAPI, left
36: 2-light PAPI, right

ASOS: 118.875
(☎727-821-4334)
Ground: 121.8
Tower:127,4

SERVICE

JET A1, 100LL
Sheltair does have courtesy cars

Bistro right on the water. It has outstanding food that you can enjoy in a genuine maritime atmosphere. The approach to the Albert Whitted Airport is an experience in and of itself because the airport is located right at the shores of the Tampa Bay and you fly entirely over water for the last few minutes. Considering the traffic density in and around Tampa, I recommend using the services of Tampa approach. They might clear you into Class B which allows you to fly higher over the water. This allows pilots to take the approach from a higher altitude because the distance over the water is quite far. If clearance for Class B is refused, then use Flight Following. This will give you a second set of eyes which really helps track air traffic, especially in busy air space. Once you've landed, FBO Sheltair gives you a friendly welcome by literally rolling out the red carpet, even for small planes. There are courtesy cars available for you to explore nearby St. Petersburg and if you refuel with at least 5 gallons of Avgas, you park your plane for free. Even if you don't refuel, you can reduce your parking fee from $10 to $5 by eating at the airport restaurant – **The Hangar**. A visit to the Hangar is worth it because from the terrace you get a great view of the incoming and outgoing air traffic from runway 07. In addition, the kitchen is open all day and well into the evening. Their breakfasts are particularly good with very generous portions.

Water or gin and tonic? It doesn't matter, the view is the same.

LINKS

www.thedali.org

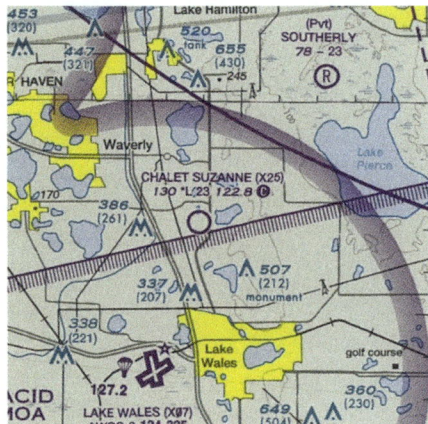

| **R W Y** | 18-36 • 2313 x 50 ft. • Grass |

| **((•))** | CTAF/UNICOM: 122.8 |

SERVICE

| **⛽** | No refueling station. |

Hard to spot from the air - the runway for Chalet Suzanne

Moon Soup is a must!

CHALET SUZANNE

Chalet Suzanne is one of those destinations that you have to work for. First, because it is not a big name destination, so it is not immediately obvious as a worthwhile stopover. Secondly, you have to find it first, which is not so easy because it's hard to find even on the sectional. It is about 4 nm northeast of Lake Wales Municipal Airport. The other reason it is hard to find is that the grass runway is difficult to see. It's best to use the town of Lake Wales as your reference point and then fly north along Highway 17, which, at this point, runs east and parallel to Interstate 27. For current weather information, I recommend the AWOS in Lake Worth (124.225).

Once you have successfully landed, you will quickly see that this is definitely one of Florida's most unique airfields, probably because the runway is just an add-on to the grounds of Chalet Suzanne.

The success of this country inn began in 1930s when it opened its doors for business as a small boarding house for travelers. Today, the family-owned and operated inn has 30 guest rooms and ranks among the top country inns in the United States. The food is outstanding, especially its Romaine Soup - also known as Moon Soup. It is famous far beyond the borders of Florida, not to mention Earth, because, as the name implies, this soup has actually been

It has been a popular destination for generations

to space. Astronaut James B. Irwin, a friend of the family, recommended the soup to his superiors, which is how it found its way to NASA and, from there, to the moon. The Apollo 15 and 16 astronauts were able to enjoy Moon Soup, as well as their Russian cosmonaut colleagues on the joint Apollo-Soyuz mission. There probably aren't many foods that have been granted such an honor. Today, Chalet Suzanne is still operated by the Hinshaw family, now in its 4th g eneration of ownership.
Oh, and the inn was named after Suzanne, the daughter of the first owner Bertha Hinshaw.

LINK
www.chaletsuzanne.com

Included in the National Register of Historic Places

83

KCGC

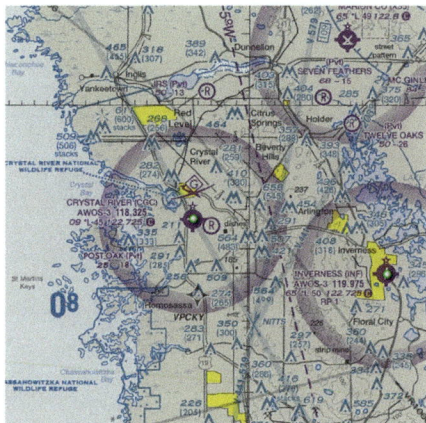

R W Y	09-27 • 4557 x 75 ft. • Asphalt 09: *2-light PAPI, left* 27: *2-light PAPI, right* 18-36 • 2666 x 100 ft. • Grass

CTAF/Unicom: 122.725
AWOS: 118.325
(☎ 352-563-6600)

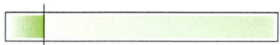

SERVICE

JET A1, 100LL

Bob's Taxi Cab ☎ 352-422-3657 or West Coast Taxi Cab
☎ 352-563-2909

Easy to see from far away

Swimming with manatees

CRYSTAL RIVER

Crystal River is a peaceful community on the Gulf of Mexico with a population of approx. 3,000, and about 14 nm northwest of Inverness on the map. This is where the largest and most accessible manatee colony in the United States can be found. The manatees mainly spend the winter months in Crystal River because it has several freshwater sources where the water is warm enough to create a comfortable habitat for these peaceful animals. Manatees are herbivorous marine mammals, and unlike seals or sea lions, are no longer able to come on land. Even though they have certain similarities to sea lions, anatomically, they are more closely related to elephants.
River Ventures and **Florida Manatee Tours** offer daily guided tours to view these marine mammals in their natural habitat. I recommend booking one of the earliest tours (6:15 am) because morning is when manatees are most playful and willing to come up close to visitors. Some are still sleeping at this time, which looks really strange because every 5 minutes, while still asleep, a manatee nose will break through the surface of the water to get air before slowly sinking back down to the bottom.
If you take a tour later in the day, the river is usually busier and what is a relaxed experience can become an obstacle course with the boat weaving its way in and out of snorkelers and kayakers.
The best time of year to see manatees is the winter because they swim toward the springs in the evening where you're almost guaranteed to run into a large herd

The animals can retire to nearby areas.

of them in the early morning. That's why I recommend doing a tour once the nights start getting cooler, though it also means that the early morning tour can be rather cold. The outerwear provided keeps you warm for a while, but even it reaches its limits at a certain point.
The starting point for tours, depending on the tour operator, is about 2 to 2.5 miles from the airport.
Another excellent tourist destination is Homasossa Springs Wildlife State Park. It covers 210 acres and is home to much of Florida's local wildlife, including, of course, manatees, who can be seen year-round in an underwater observatory. The park is also home to snakes, black bears, crocodiles, alligators, red foxes, otters and much more. It's about a 10-minute drive to the park.
Just one mile from the airport is the

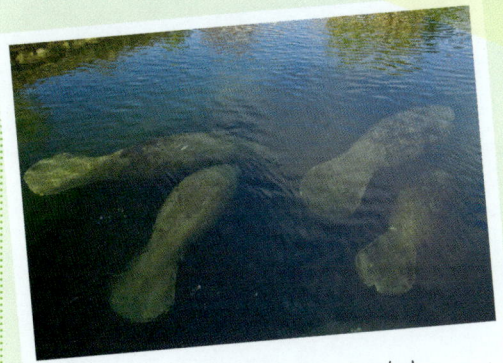

The manatees swim into the bay to eat

7 Rivers Golf & Country Club, which is now also open to non-members.
Also, it's about a 10-minute walk from the airport to the usual chain restaurants like Applebee's, Dairy Queen, Chili's. The airport does not have a restaurant.

Stranded Piper Super Cub

A flight over the area is worth it

LINKS

www.riverventures.com
www.floridamanateetours.calls.net
www.7riversgolf.com

Sufficient parking
for everyone

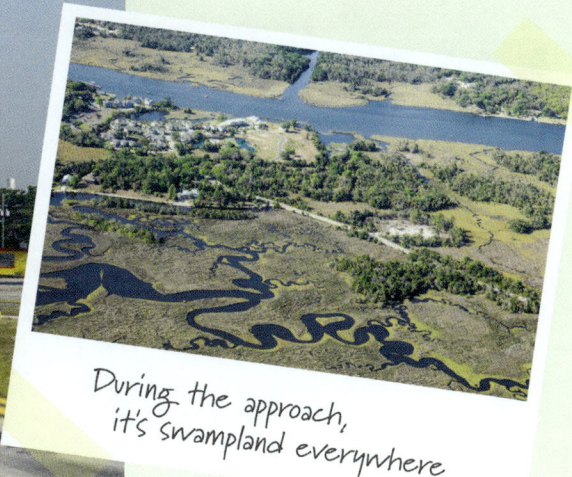

During the approach,
it's swampland everywhere

KDED

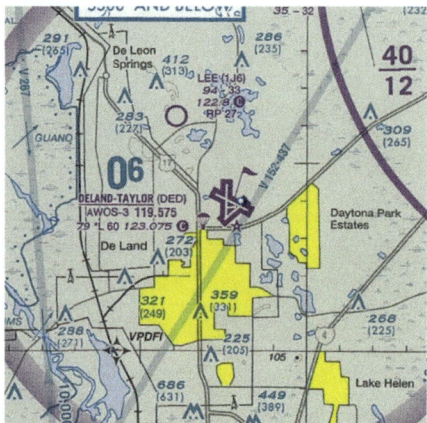

R W Y
05-23 • 4301 x 75 ft.
2-light PAPI, left

12-30 • 6001 x 100 ft.
12: 2-light PAPI, left
30: 4-light PAPI, left

CTAF/UNICOM: 123.075
AWOS: 119.575
(☎ 386-740-5811)

SERVICE

JET A1, 100LL

Rental car:
enterprise ☎ 386-738-4013

Taxi: Orange Cab
☎386-734-0545,
Lucas Cab ☎386-734-2401

Not for the faint of heart

DELAND MUNICIPAL-SIDNEY H TAYLOR FIELD AIRPORT

If you're interested in skydiving then you shouldn't miss DeLand. It is **the** place for skydiving in Florida and one of the leading centers in the USA. But this also

LINKS

www.skydivedeland.com
www.airportginmill.com

means that you have to be particularly careful during take-off and landing in order to avoid getting in the way of skydivers or their jump planes. Flyovers over the airport should be avoided and active radio communication is highly recommended.

The skydiving school **Skydive DeLand** also has its own pub called **The Perfect Spot** right on site. The FBO does not have much to offer, though there is a good view of the skydiver landing point. Right near the FBO is the **Airport Restaurant and Gin Mill**. Here, you can enjoy a meal on the patio right next to the ramp. Sometimes there is also live music. The **DeLand Jet Center** offers customers a courtesy car so you can explore the area. The downtown has its own Historic Garden District. If you want to stay a while, you can also arrange for a rental car from enterprise.

KXFL

Wings at Highjackers Restaurant

FLAGLER COUNTY AIRPORT

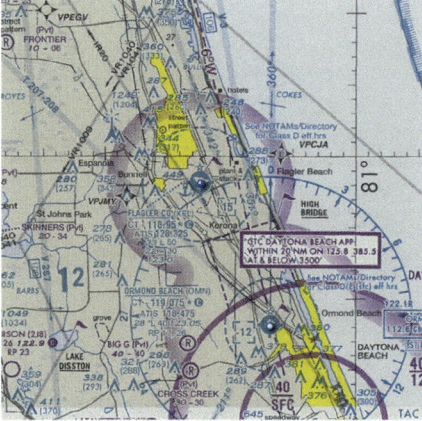

The town of Flagler was named after Henry Morrison Flagler, who played a major role in the development of Florida's east coast. He not only owned the Florida East Coast Railway, which in its heyday, ran a rail line all the way to Key West and is still in operation today, he is also considered a founding father of Palm Beach and Miami. Right next to the FBO is one of the

RWY
06-24 • 5000 x 100 ft.
2-light PAPI, left
11-29 • 4999 x 100 ft.
2-light PAPI, left

((•)) ATIS: 128.325 (☎386-437-7334)
Ground: 121.75
Tower: 118.95

SERVICE

⛽ JET A1, 100LL
Rental cars: enterprise

most famous airport restaurants in Florida: **Highjackers**. Like so many successful airport restaurants, Highjackers has also been able to attract customers outside of the pilot community. If you fly in for lunch, you may be enjoying the company of not only other pilots, but contractors and nurses, who are taking their lunch break here. This mix of clientele makes it a nice place to eat and spend time. However, the atmosphere clearly reflects a passion for aviation. The patio seating is practically right on the apron, so that you always have a good view of air traffic. The service is excellent and friendly and the chicken wings are legendary. It is a must-do for

any visit to Florida. However, Flagler and Highjackers are no longer well-kept secrets. So plan ahead. The airport ranks among the most frequented areas for general air traffic in Florida.
Though the FBO at Flagler County Airport does not offer courtesy cars, you can, if needed, get a taxi (Flagler Beach is 5 miles from the airport). If required, the friendly staff at the FBO will also help you find overnight accommodation.

LINK
www.highjackers.com

Wild Air Boat Tours

INVERNESS AIRPORT

R W Y	01-19 • 5001 x 75 ft. 4-light PAPI, right

CTAF/UNICOM: 122.725 AWOS: 119.975

SERVICE

JET A1, 100LL
Airport Taxi: 352-201-9828

Wild Bill's jetty

Surrounded by lakes, the city of Inverness is located at the junction of SR44, which crosses the city east-west and the SR41, which runs north-south. The airport is located in the southwest quadrant of this junction, directly next to the Speedway course which is easy to see from the air. Except for the FBO, there isn't much there. The nearest restaurant is about a 10-minute walk appr. a mile north in the direction of Inverness. It's called **Peppermint Patties New England & Southern Seafood Restaurant** (Tel. +1 352-419-4878). This restaurant, as the name implies, offers genuine New England style cooking. Also, about a 10-15 minute drive from the airport is the starting point for **Wild Bill's Airboat Tours**. In a one-hour boat tour, you can discover Florida's primordial landscape and learn all there is to know about the Withlacoochee River, which runs 150 miles north right through Florida. You will usually see alligators (though never guaranteed), but also turtles, ospreys, owls, falcons and sometimes even bears. It's a fun tour, especially for families. Because the motor boat's 600 HP engine can get fairly loud, hearing protection is provided. At the end of the tour, most tour guides don't bother turning off the Chevy engines while maneuvering the flatbed boat into the slip. To avoid getting wet, it's best to choose a seat away from the edge of the boat toward the middle. Tip: If you book online, you'll get a discount from $45 to $35 for adults.

Difficult to see for untrained eyes

LINKS

www.wildbillsairboattour.com
www.fishermansflorida.com

Such wildlife adventures make for a big appetite. Directly across from Wild Bill's, on the other side of the road, is the **Fishermans Restaurant**, specializing in fish and other seafood. It has a family-friendly atmosphere and is reasonably priced. It is closed on Mondays and Tuesdays.

Fast ride through wild swampland area

KISM

LASER LIGHT ACTIVITY
See Airport/Facility Directory

R W Y	15-33 • 6001 x 100 ft.
	4-light PAPI, left
	06-24 • 5001 x 150 ft.
	4-light PAPI, left

ATIS: 128.775
Ground: 121.7
Tower: 124.45

SERVICE

JET A1, 100LL

Transport: courtesy cars, National, enterprise, Hertz, AVIS

There is a lot of air traffic around Orlando, which means keep your eyes open.

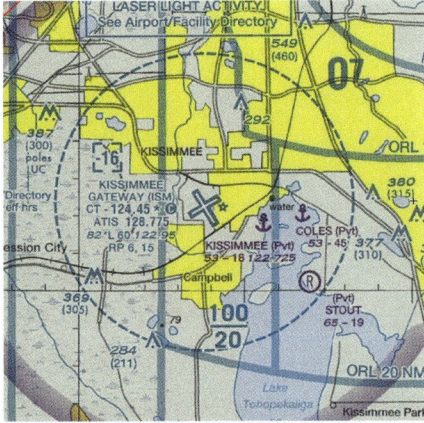

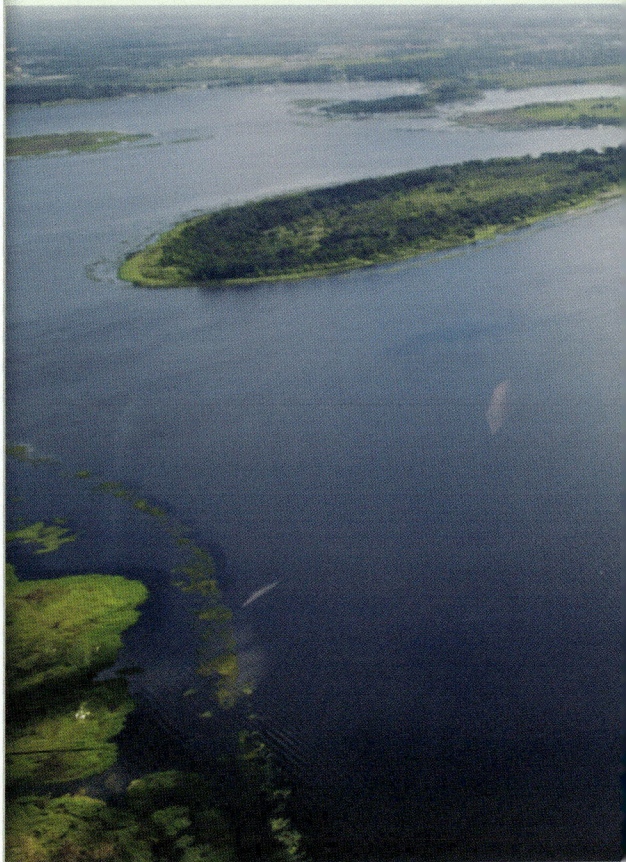

The Gateway to Disney

KISSIMMEE GATEWAY AIRPORT

The Kissimmee Gateway Airport is the nearest airport to the many Disney attractions. Although it is a truly busy area, the atmosphere is relatively relaxed. The tower controllers are very friendly and are used to dealing with visitors who are unfamiliar with the airport. The two long crossed

runways make landing possible with little crosswind. When approaching, pay attention to Orlando air space B and the temporary flight restrictions (TFR) over Disney. This TFR has been in effect since 9/11 and considered by many as a permanent flight restriction mainly because it has been continuously active for years. If you are flying with flight following, you can request clearance into Orlando Class B, which the controllers usually give as long as the air space is not too congested. There are three major FBOs at this airport that all offer outstanding services. We have used the services of **Kissimmee Jet Centers** because its price for Avgas is reasonable. As far as facilities go, it's not as elegant as the other FBOs who mainly target business customers. We arrived in the Jet Center without advance notice and had a rental car within 10 minutes. All FBOs offer courtesy cars free of charge, but they can only be used for a limited period of time (about 1.5 hours). If you plan on going to Disney World, I recommend getting your own rental car or simply going by taxi.

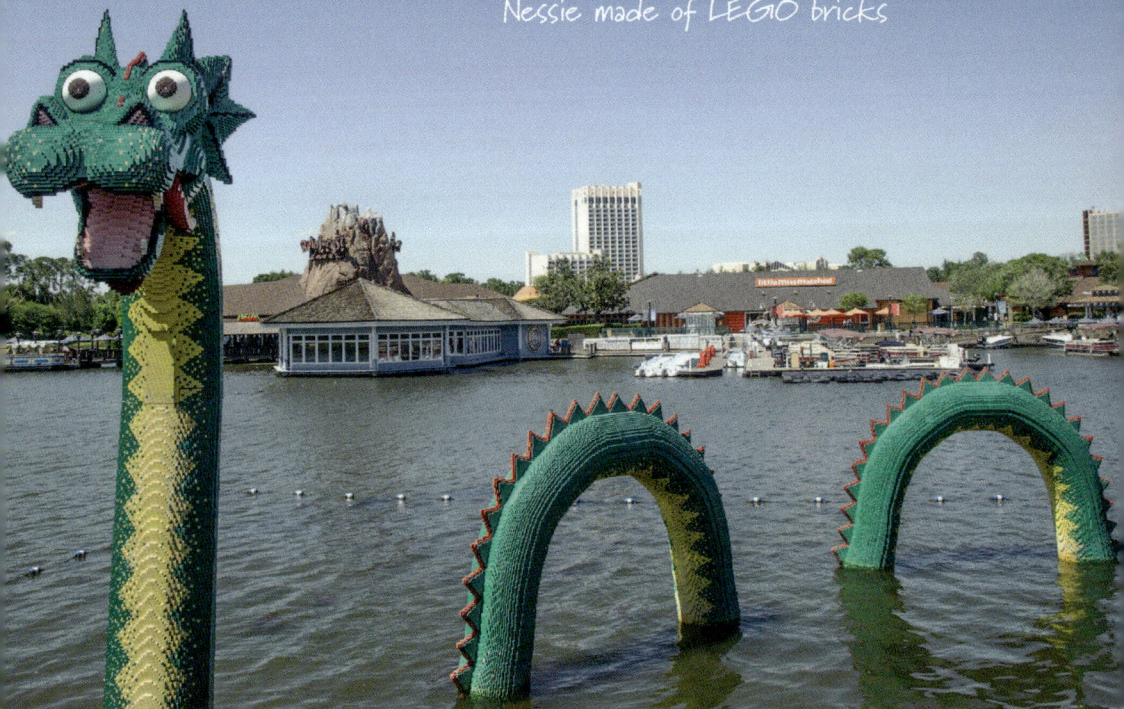

Nessie made of LEGO bricks

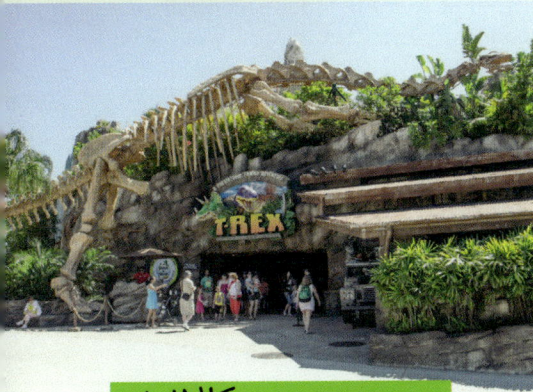

LINK
wdtc.disneyinternational.com/

It's about a 15-minute drive from the airport to get to the first Disney attractions. There is just too much to see and do at Disney World to include in this guide, so I recommend buying a separate travel guide for Disney World. But if you want to get an idea of what Disney World is like, then try heading to **Downtown Disney**. This is an area open to the public where you don't have to pay an entrance fee. There are shops, restaurants, cafés and all kinds of other Disney-related attractions. There you can find **Cirque du Soleil**, **La Nouba**, **Disney Quest**, **The House of Blues**, **Planet Hollywood**, and, more recently, a **LEGO Imagination Center**, **World of Disney**, and much more. One of the main attractions is the **Empress Lilly** building, which now is home to **Fulton's Crab House**. It is an imitation of the old Mississippi style paddle steamer river boats, but is not really a boat, rather it rests on an underwater concrete bedplate. If all this makes you want to see more, then take one of the many shuttles from Downtown Disney to other attractions.

You can buy LEGO here to build your own Nessie

KLAL

| R W Y | 05-23 • 5005 x 150 ft. *4-light PAPI, left* 09-27 • 8499 x 150 ft. *09: 4-light PAPI, right* *27: 4-light PAPI, left* |

ATIS: 118.025
Tower: 124.5
Ground: 121.4

SERVICE

JET A1, 100LL
Taxi: Checker Cab
☎863-665-8151,
Shuttle Services
☎863-712-3775

LAKELAND LINDER REGIONAL AIRPORT

Lakeland Linder Regional Airport is known far and wide as the organizer of the world's second largest aviation event called **SUN 'n FUN** International Fly-in and Expo. Each year in April, pilots from all over the United States along with about 4,000 aircrafts fly into Lakeland to learn about the newest products from the show's 500 exhibitors or to attend a few of the nearly 450 forums, seminars and work-shops held there. During the event, air shows are held twice a day, during which Warbirds, Wing Walkers and aerobatic aircraft perform breath-taking maneuvers and aerobatics. Its mix of educational events, new products and air shows and, of course, meeting other aviation enthusiasts makes this event an unfor-gettable experience.

Replica of a SE-5A

Nestled in the woods –
the SUN 'n FUN complex

LINK
www.sun-n-fun.org

If you want to spend the night
in Lakeland, you can check in
right across the street.

The calm
before the storm

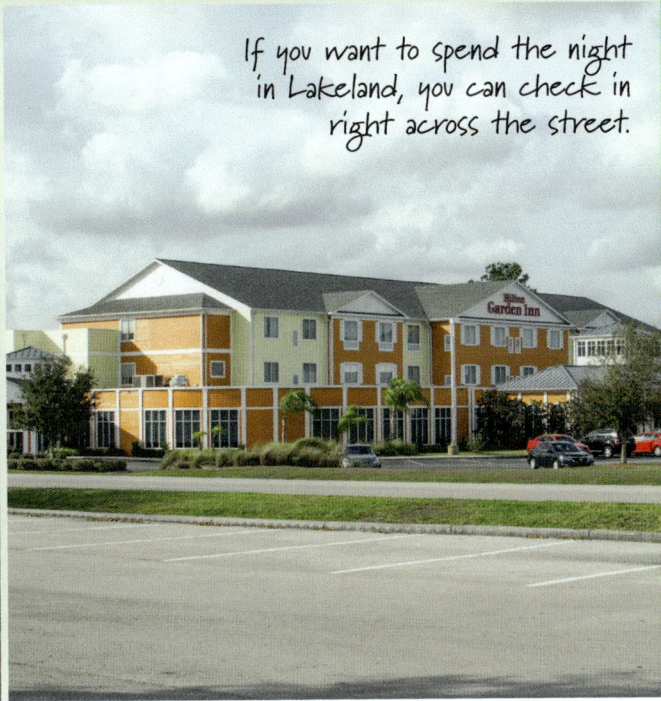

Every day, Warbirds fly in the most diverse formations

WW II classic planes to marvel at

On some days, there is a shortage of shade

There is no fear of mixing old and new

The rest of the year in Lakeland is a bit quieter. On the first floor of the terminal building is **Earhart's Café**, which is only open at lunchtime on Mondays and Tuesdays, but is otherwise open from 11:00 a.m. onwards. The café has a great view of the runway and, as a special feature, it has several headsets available so you can listen in on ATIS, Ground and Tower. Lakeland is also headquarters to **Breezer Aircraft USA**, which charters several planes.

Across from the terminal building are the SUN 'n FUN grounds and the SUN 'n FUN Museum. There are several exhibits from all eras of aviation, starting from the beginning of the 20th century. Business hours:

MO-FR: 9:00 a.m. -5:00 p.m.

SA 10:00 a.m.-4:00 p.m.,

SU 12:00 p.m. - 4:00 p.m.

Right next door is the **PilotMall.com** which is one of the largest pilot stores in all of Florida.

Cockpit of a WW II liasion aircraft

SUN 'n FUN SPECIAL

Start of a new air show

Everyday classics

Central Lake County

| R W Y | 18-36 • 3200 x 80 ft. |

| (•) | CTAF/UNICOM: 122.8
ASOS Leesburg: 134,325 |

SERVICE

No refueling station.

The grass runway is very bumpy

Central Lake County

MID FLORIDA AIR SERVICE AIRPORT

About 9 nm east of Leesburg International located in central Lake County is the sleepy grassy field runway of Mid Florida. The airfield is privately owned, but remains open for public use. However, please note that there is no fuel station here. In contrast to some publications on the Internet, the fuel station here was shut down several years ago. The runway itself is bumpy so be careful. From here, you can head toward Eustis (5 miles) as well as Mt. Dora (10 miles) or Tavares (10 miles). If you can't get a ride to town with one of the local pilots, you can call the Eustis Taxis (Tel.: 352-357-3671).

Tavares is home to the Tavares Seaplane Base **Jones Brothers Seaplane Adventures** which offers flight training but also seaplane sightseeing tours.

Right behind Jones Brothers is the historic **Orange Blossom Cannonball** steam train whose station is located about 200 yards from the flight school. This lovingly restored old steam train operates primarily on the weekends. A ride on the Orange Blossom Cannonball is not just a highlight for steam train fans, but for anyone who just wants to sit in the same train that once carried famous actors like Natalie Wood, Robert Redford, Charles Bronson, Patrick Swayze, Jodi Foster, Olivia de Havilland, Rachael Leigh Cook or George Clooney – to name just a few.

Orange Blossom
Cannonball Train

A true alternative to Winter Haven

LINK

www.orangeblossomcannonball.com

KEVB

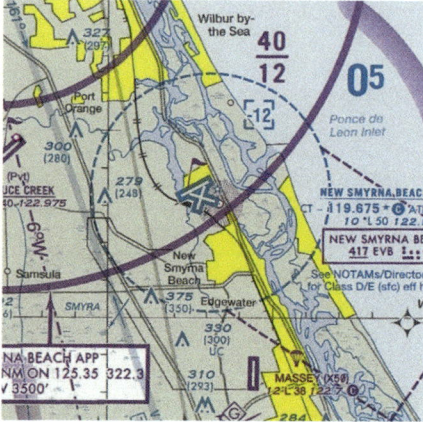

R W Y	07-25 • 5000 x 75 ft. 11-29 • 4319 x 100 ft. *4-light PAPI, left* 02-20 • 4000 x 100 ft. *4-light PAPI, left*

ATIS: 124.625
AWOS: 124.625 (☎386-409-4705)
Ground: 121.325
Tower: 119.675

SERVICE

JET A1, 100LL
Transport: enterprise, AVIS

NEW SMYRNA BEACH MUNICIPAL AIRPORT

New Smyrna Beach is one of the oldest settlements in Florida. It was founded in 1768 by Scottish physician Dr. Andrew Turnbull, who brought 1,500 settlers from the Mediterranean to Florida all in one go, making him the first ever to attempt establishing a settlement of this size before. Many of the settlers came from Smyrna, now called Izmir in Turkey, which is where the town got its name. The settlement did not last long due to various diseases that plagued the settlers as well as Dr. Turnbull's strict rules and regulations. Moreover, the Seminole natives made life hard for the settlers so that many of them moved to St. Augustine in 1777. Turnbull himself also left the colony and retired to Charleston, North Carolina.

Today, New Smyrna Beach is a lively community with a population of roughly 20,000. It has some of the most beautiful sandy beaches on the east coast. However, be careful when swimming because there have been more shark attacks here than anywhere else in the world, earning it the nickname "World's Shark Bite Capital."

The New Smyrna Beach Municipal Airport is located directly on Highway 1, which goes up and down the entire Florida east coast until ending finally in Key West.

There are three fuel stations located at the airport, one of them is operated by

LINK

www.daytonainternationalspeedway.com

the airport itself. **Airgate Aviation** and **Epic Aviation** are also two classic FBOs, though Epic is more of a flight school. Airgate operates a very small, somewhat hidden café, **Airgate Café**, directly at the airport. Coming from the runway, you will see it on the left side of the large Airgate Hangar. Both FBOs offer rental cars and courtesy cars, thus making it easy to take a quick trip to the beach where there are also a few seafood restaurants.

The airport at New Smyrna Beach is also a base point for a trip to Daytona if you'd prefer not landing directly in Daytona between various airliners. Daytona is the main venue for NASCAR racing and is famous for its wild Spring Break party season. Both are undoubtedly great fun. You can see the racetrack clearly from the air if Daytona tower gives you a midfield crossing.

Ready for the next flight

KOCF

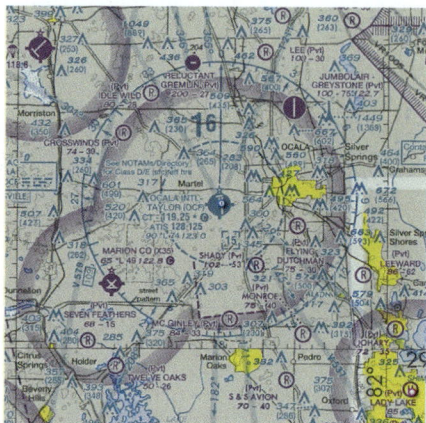

R W Y	18-38 • 7467 x 150 ft. *4-light PAPI, left* 08-26 • 3009 x 50 ft.

ATIS: 128.125
Ground: 121.4
Tower: 119.25

SERVICE

JET A1, 100LL

OCALA INTL AIRPORT JIM TAYLOR FIELD

Though the name Ocala International Airport suggests a busy international airport, it is one of the quieter airports compared to the considerably busier ones up and down Florida's east coast. Nevertheless or perhaps because of this, its services are very good. **Landmark Aviation** is an outstanding FBO and many locals argue that the burgers at the airport restaurant **Tailwind Café** are the best in Florida.
If you fly in from the northwest, you

It's rarely crowded here.

can see John Travolta's house and the Jumbolair – Greystone private airfield at 8 nm.

The house is located at the eastside of the runway, right in the middle. Here, Travolta is able to land his Boeing 707 on the 7500 ft (!) long runway, which was not possible at his previous home in Spruce Creek.

A rare sight: Most people here rather fly a Cessna or similar sized aircraft.

KPCM

R W Y	10-28 • 3948 x 75 ft. • Asphalt *2-light PAPI, left*

(((•)))	CTAF/UNICOM: 123.05 AWOS: 120.025 (☎813-764-8259)

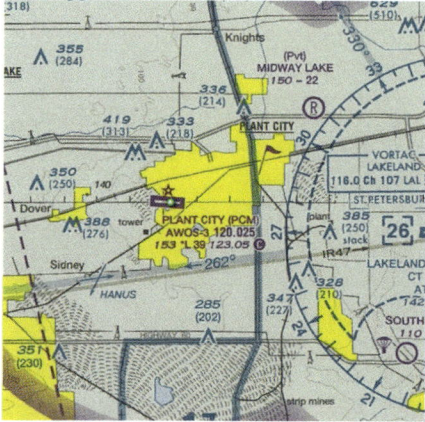

SERVICE

⛽	JET A1, 100LL

Rental car:
enterprise ☎813-752-4255

Taxi: United Cab ☎813-253-2424,
Dial-A-Ride ☎813-752-5255

Strawberry capital of the USA

PLANT CITY AIRPORT

Plant City has roughly 30,000 inhabitants and is located between Tampa and Lakeland. Plant City was originally called Ichepucksassa, a name that created so much confusion that it changed its name to Cork, and then to Plant City, to honor Henry B. Plant, the man who brought the railroad to Plant City.

The Plant City Airport is one of the quieter airports in central Florida, except during the Strawberry Festival and the Sun n' Fun Fly-in.

This area is home to the largest strawberry growing region in the United States and to honor it, the city holds a huge strawberry festival once a year. This event transforms

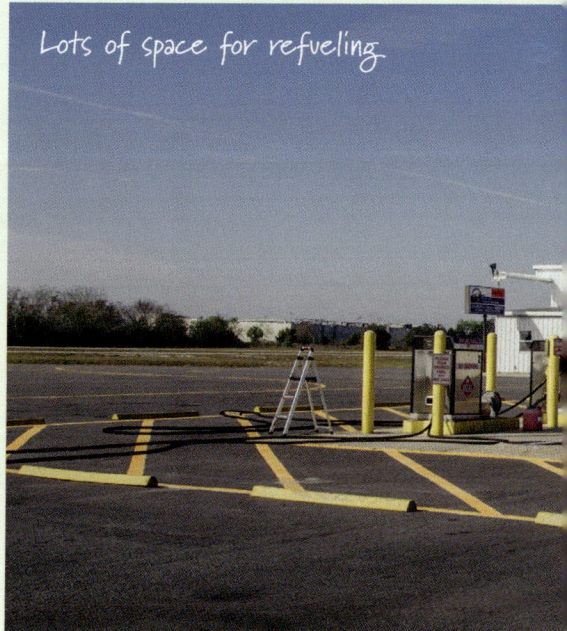

Lots of space for refueling

the otherwise quiet town into an exceptionally busy and active place. Over several days, there are live concerts, tours and a huge folk festival. Of course, the local strawberry queen is also crowned. If you don't want to miss the strawberry festival, then make sure you reserve accommodation and concert tickets well in advance.

Landing in Plant City is also a good option if you want to avoid Lakeland and its higher prices during Sun 'n Fun as well as a 12-page NOTAM for your approach. For the short trip to Lakeland by car, I recommend either reserving a car from enterprise in advance or calling the local taxi. It's about 7 miles from Lakeland to Plant City.

In addition, Plant City is a good alternative to Tampa if you want to avoid its busy airport. It's about a half hour drive into the downtown.

Private aviation is more common in Plant City

LINK
www.flstrawberryfestival.com

2RR

RIVER RANCH RESORT AIRPORT

| R W Y | 16-34 • 4950 x 75 ft. |

| (((•))) | CTAF/UNICOM: 122.8 |

SERVICE

| ⛽ | JET A1, 100LL |

Golf carts are available right at the airport

The River Ranch Resort Airport is in a wooded area, making it relatively difficult to identify when you are flying low on your way to River Ranch. A canal that runs east and parallel to the landing strip is a good reference point. Due to the adjacent trees, air turbulence often occurs on final. Make sure you respect the right traffic pattern for runway 34.

River Ranch is a terrific destination for the entire family. You can also plan a vacation here or even reserve for a long weekend. Accommodation options range from simple double rooms to self-catering cabins. You'll notice right way here that it is no longer a real ranch with tilled fields and pastures with grazing cattle, rather this is a true resort operated by Westgate.

If you don't plan to stay overnight, it's best to rent a golf cart to take a quick tour of the grounds. You can pick it up right at the runway and pay just $5 for 2.5 hours. The ranch is situated over a large area that includes a mobile home park, a golf course (9 holes) and a marina. There are plenty of places on the ranch to enjoy a good meal or snack. From the airport, it's a 5 minute drive with the golf cart to the **Westgate Smokehouse Grill** at the other end of the street. It is open daily. There is also a pier where airboats can dock. Unlike its predecessors from the wild west, the **River Ranch Saloon**

Entrance to the ranch – not everyone gets on their high horse

Mobile home instead of wooden cabin

opens its swinging doors only on Fridays through Sunday evening. There is often live music, and dance classes are held there.

The Ranch offers a plethora of outdoor recreational activities, including golf, air boat tours, horseback riding and clay pigeon shooting. One event not to miss is the rodeo evening held on Saturdays.

LINK
www.wgriverranch.com

7FL6

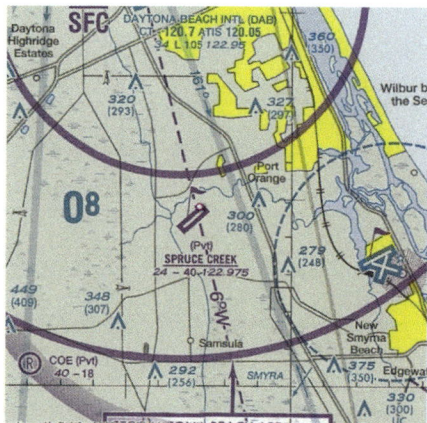

R W Y	05-23 • 4000 x 176 ft.
	2-light PAPI, left

UNICOM: 122.975

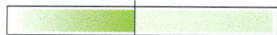

SERVICE

JET A1, 100LL

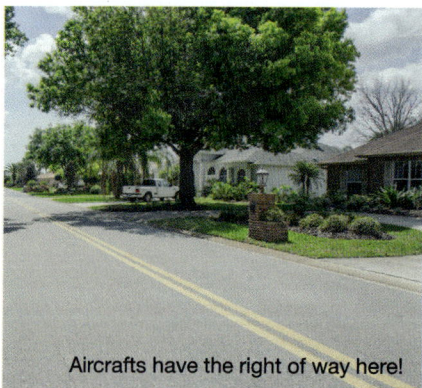

Aircrafts have the right of way here!

SPRUCE CREEK

What pilot hasn't dreamed of having his airplane parked right next to his house, with just a few hundred yards to taxi to the runway and up in the air you go! That's what it's like every day at the Spruce Creek residential airpark community, which is one of the oldest and finest aviation communities in the USA and has always served as a model for others. The community became well-known when its most famous resident, John Travolta lived there. Unfortunately, he had to move after acquiring a Boeing 707 because it was too big to land in Spruce Creek. Today, Spruce Creek is a lively aviator community that does not cut itself off, like many others. Visitors are allowed to land for a flying visit. Please park in the parking areas marked especially for guests. If you want to stay overnight, you need an invitation from a member of the community. There are no guestrooms or cottages for rent here. For Spruce Creek to continue to remain open for visitors, please follow the rules of conduct that are posted on the community's website. As long as you follow them, there is nothing to stop you from taking a nice stroll through this fabulous dream fly-in community. Lastly, you should fill your own tank at the local airport restaurant next to the FBO before heading back to the harsh reality of the real world. It's best to fly into Spruce Creek either from the north directly over the Daytona International Airport or from the coast through the VFR corridor. More details can be found on the website.

LINK

www.fly-in.com/creek_arrival-dep.html
www.fly-in.com/index.html

The hangar is located right
next to the house — perfect.

There is no traffic jam here

The street is a taxiway

KTIX

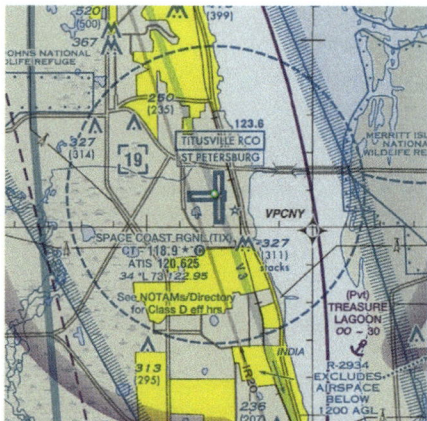

TITUSVILLE - SPACE COAST REGIONAL AIRPORT

| R W Y | 18-36 • 7319 x 150 ft. *4-light PAPI, left* |
| | 9-27 • 5000 x 100 ft. *4-light PAPI, left* |

ATIS: 120.625
Tower: 118.9
Ground: 121.85

SERVICE

JET A1, 100LL
Bristow Air Center und Space Coast Jet Center

Titusville should be your first choice destination for a visit to the **John F. Kennedy Space Center**. When approaching you can see the Kennedy Space Center about 6 miles away as the crow flies. To get there, I recommend calling a taxi from the FBO, it's about a 25-minute drive. A tour of the John F. Kennedy Space Center has certainly got to be one of the highlights of a visit to Florida. So make sure you plan in enough time for it. If you prefer a quick visit and don't mind missing a few exhibits, you can make it through in 2-3 hours, but it is better to schedule a whole day. At any rate, it's best to check out the website ahead of time. It also lists the current opening hours which tend to vary at different times of the year. Lastly, the website displays the countdown to the next rocket launch that you can track from different areas around the Space Center. A ticket is not required for this.

Next Launch T-Minus: 6 D : 00 : 29 : 17 EST

If an entire day in space is too much for you, I recommend a visit to the Warbird

LINK

www.kennedyspacecenter.com

Entrance to the FBO

Newly restored radial engine

Almost all aircraft exhibited are airworthy.

Museum, located at the airport, as an alternative. To do so, it's best to park at the **Bristow Air Center** and walk about 15 minutes north to the museum. **The Valiant Air Command Warbird Museum** has exhibits from the Second World War as well as the Vietnam War. Many of the old machines are still airworthy and are either flown privately (on loan) or for air shows. From smaller models such as the Tiger Moth or a Piper Cub to fighter jets and even the C47 Dakota, if you are a passionate fan of Warbirds, you won't be disappointed. Among the aircraft on exhibit, there is also a B-25B Mitchell, displayed just as it was on April 18, 1942 during the Doolittle Raid on Tokyo.

First fueling after a long restoration

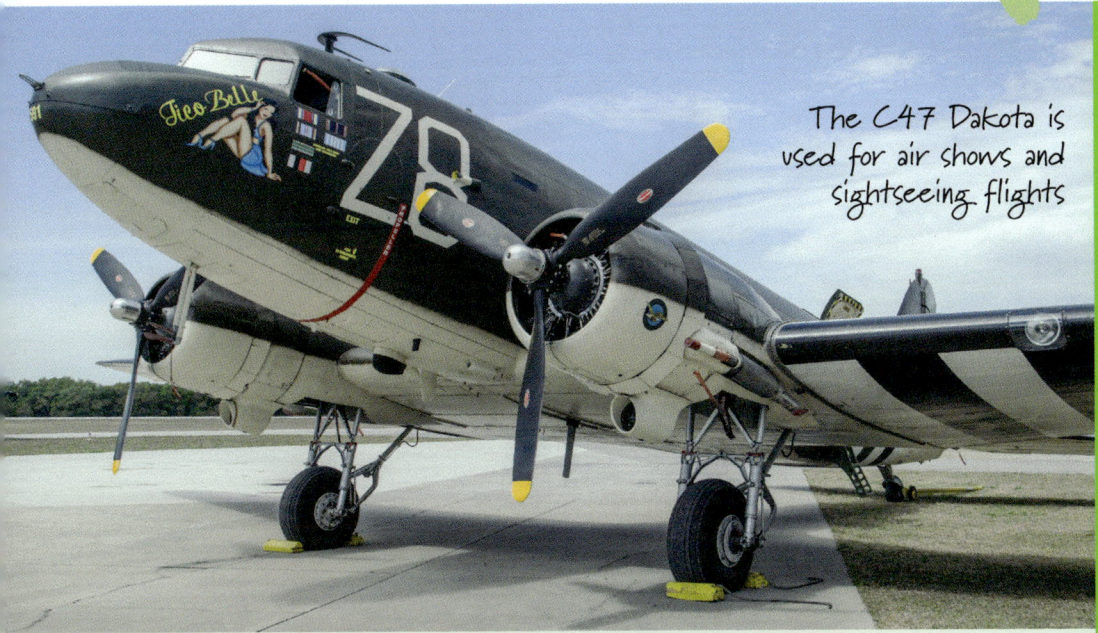

The C47 Dakota is used for air shows and sightseeing flights

Parking in front of the Warbird Museum

Who hasn't heard of the Blue Angels?

119

KGIF

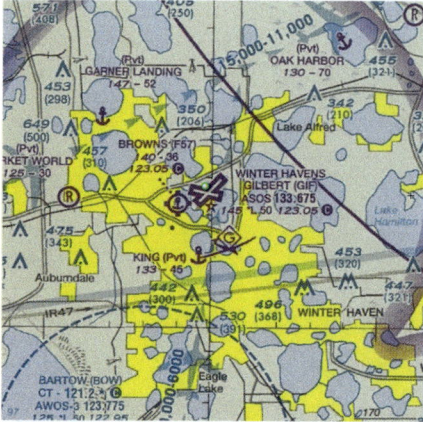

R W Y	05-23 • 5005 x 100 ft. *2-light PAPI, left* 11-29 • 4001 x 100 ft.

ASOS: 133.675
CTAF/UNICOM: 123.05

SERVICE

JET A1, 100LL
Taxi: Winter Haven
☎863-324-9166

WINTER HAVEN MUNICIPAL AIRPORT GILBERT FIELD

Nestled in a maze of lakes deep in the heart of Florida is Winter Haven, also about 15 nm west of Lakeland. The Winter Haven Municipal Airport is the ideal destination for many reasons. The airport itself also has a few perks to offer. The FBO **Hova Flight Services** is an extremely helpful FBO. It operates simultaneously as a flight school, Tecnam service provider and sales partner. There is also **Pappy's Grill** which is located in the airport building. Here you can find classic American dishes from 7:00 a.m. to 2:00 p.m. and if you eat here, you'll get a $.20 discount on fuel. The area around Winter Haven also has quite a lot to offer.

About 13 miles north of here is a great attraction for the entire family: **Fantasy Of Flight**. It is the world's largest private collection of classic planes with over 100 aircraft, many of which are still in good enough condition to fly. You can see for yourself at the air shows held daily, during which the owner of the collection, Kermit Weeks, often flies himself. You can also gaze at rare aircraft like the Boeing B-17G Flying Fortress, the Consolidated PBY-5A Catalina or the North American P-51D Mustang. All aircraft can be seen close up. You can even go inside and sit in the cockpit of some of them. The maintenance shops give visitors a good look at how

Parking for seaplanes

LINKS

www.brownsseaplane.com
www.fantasyofflight.com
florida.legoland.com

planes are restored. But you can also learn something about flying. For example, if you ever wanted to fly a Boeing Stearman yourself, you can do it here. If you're done marveling at the aircraft, why not head over to the Wing WalkAir ropes course and zipline. Unfortunately, the airport that belongs to the museum called Orlampa (Identifier FA08) is not open to the public.

Located about 10 miles southeast of the airport is **LEGOLAND Florida,** another attraction for the entire family. Actually, it's two attractions, LEGOLAND and the LEGOLAND Water Park. You should plan on one whole day to visit both. Directly next to the airport is **Jack Brown's Seaplane Base** where seaplane pilots have undergone training since 1963.

Already 17,000 seaplane ratings have been issued here.

The FBO goes electric

KZPH

R W Y	04-22 • 4999 x 100 ft. *4-light PAPI, left*
	18-36 • 4954 x 100 ft. *4-light PAPI, left*

CTAF/Unicom: 123.075
ASOS: 118.975 (☎813-780-0031)

SERVICE

JET A1, 100LL

Mix of thrift store and Café

ZEPHYRHILLS MUNICIPAL AIRPORT

Like so many other airports in Florida, the Zephyrhills Municipal Airport can look back on a military past. This is where fighter pilots were trained for missions back in the 1940's. Located right near the FBO is the **World War II Barracks Museum**, which is open on weekends and has items from this era on display. Parked in front of the museum is a Douglas C53D, which is currently being restored.

The grounds cover over 7000 acres and were given to the city of Zephyrhills after the war and it has operated the airport ever since. Nowadays, the airport mainly handles general aviation traffic and is used as a base for skydiving. It only gets really hectic once a year when the Sun'n Fun Festival is held in neighboring Lakeland in April because it is used as an alternative landing airport when it gets too busy at Lakeland. There are shuttles available for transport between the two airports.

The FBO has courtesy cars available for a maximum of 1.5 hours. I recommend driving right to **Flaco's**, a Cuban restaurant popular among pilots and only a few minutes away by car.

Neighboring Dade City has several beautifully restored historic buildings.

A visit to **Mallie Kyla's Café** should not be missed. It is located downtown and is a garish mix between café and thrift store. It is known for its homemade

The Pasco County Court House

cooking. The desserts here are highly recommended. For longer day trips, you can reserve a rental car from enterprise.

During the approach, make sure you keep an eye out for skydivers. Zephyrhills is one of the oldest skydiving centers in the United States.

LINK

www.skydivecity.com

Douglas C53D at the World War II Barracks Museum

This is an exception – 95% of all flights are small aircraft

123

SOUTH

- Everglades Airpark, Everglades City
- Fort Lauderdale Executive Airport
- Kendall-Tamiami Executive Airport
- Key West International Airport
- Marco Island Executive Airport
- Naples Municipal Airport
- Okeechobee County Airport
- Page Field Airport, Fort Myers
- Palm Beach County Park Airport
- The Florida Keys Marathon Airport
- Venice Municipal Airport
- Vero Beach Municipal Airport

FLORIDA

XØ1

EVERGLADES AIRPARK, EVERGLADES CITY

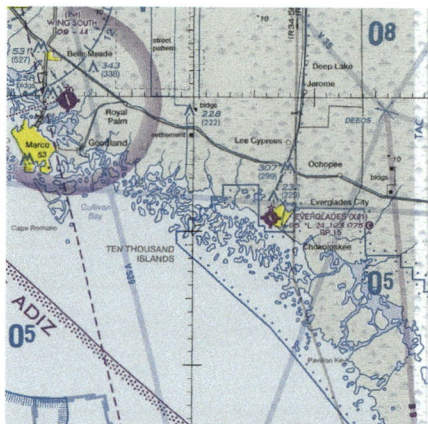

RWY	15-33 • 2400 x 60 ft.

(((•)))	CTAF/UNICOM: 123.075 AWOS in KMKY (18 nm NW): 120.075 (☎ 239-394-8187)

SERVICE

⛽	JET A1, 100LL

The Everglades Airpark lies in the middle of the 10,000 Islands Region. It's easy to see from the air where this region got its name from. This unique landscape made up of thousands of small islands stretches over a distance of 25 nm - starting with Marco Island to several miles south of Everglades City. If you're lucky enough to fly over this labyrinth at sunset, you will be treated to a light show, the likes of which you will never have seen before. With a runway length of just 2400 ft, Everglades Airpark has one of the shortest runways in Florida. Even if most European pilots are used to such short runway lengths, it's better to err on the side of caution because its proximity to the sea and a group of trees to the west can cause windy surprises. Once on the ground, this airfield will seem like the last outpost of civilization, which is rather unusual for Florida. There are no traffic lights or taxis. Golf courses or shopping malls? That's a negative! Instead, you can experience nature at its purest with all kinds of outdoor recreational activities. The FBO has brochures and fliers from most of the local tour companies and tourist attractions. I recommend picking a place first, because this then determines whether you will

turn right or left at the end of the road leading out of the airport. Some airboat operators and restaurants also provide a

Aircraft are secured against the wind and strapped down

Expect crosswind here

shuttle service, which can be a good option depending on your sense of adven-ture, especially during the hotter time of year. Turning left takes you into town, turning right takes you to the **Everglades National Park**, to **Glades Haven Marina** and to the **Oyster House**. It's about a

Sunset over 10,000 islands

Last rays of light over the 10,000 islands

Boats, kayaks and delicious food

10-minute walk to get there. Boat tours start from the **Everglades National Park** and take about 1.5 to almost 2 hours. The Ten Thousand Islands Tour starts at about 9:30 a.m. and runs hourly until about 5:00 p.m. The Mangrove Wilderness Tour starts from 9:00 a.m. and runs about every other hour until 3:30 p.m. (9:30 a.m., 11:00 a.m., 11:30 a.m., 1:00 p.m., 1:30 p.m. 3:00 p.m., 3:30 p.m.). Ranging in price from $30 to $40, these tours are not exactly cheap, but they are definitely a genuine experience. If you'd prefer exploring the region on your own, you can rent kayaks or motor boats at the **Glades Haven Marina**. However, the motor boats are rented out only on a day basis, not per hour. If you want a snack before heading out on a tour, the place to go is the **Oyster House** which serves all kinds of seafood as well as steaks. I highly recommend trying the stone crab, which is found mainly in the Gulf of Mexico, or alligator. Located right next to the restaurant is a wooden observation tower where you get a great view of the Mangrove landscape. If you walk out of the airport and take a left, you'll reach a main traffic intersection after about 15-20 minutes where you'll see the Everglades City town hall at the north end of town. Take a right at the intersection and after a few minutes, you'll see the **Raw Bar** restaurant, a rustic structure built on stilts where you can enjoy refreshments right on the water. Boats belonging to several airboat tour operators are also moored here. Right

next door is the **Seafood Depot**. Back at the main intersection, if you turn left and then take an immediate right onto N Storter Ave, you'll come to the **Triad Seafood Café** after about 10 minutes. This restaurant also has a patio right on the water. Some guests arrive here by boat or seaplane. The Triad is very popular and well-known beyond Everglades City. It's best to call in advance to check opening times and to reserve a table. (+1 239 695 0722). You can also request pick-up at the airport. It is always worth asking! Held each year at the beginning of February is the **Everglades Seafood Festival**, an event that's not to be missed. For exact dates, see the below website.

LINKS

www.evergladesseafoodfestival.org
triadseafoodmarketcafe.com
www.captaindougs.net

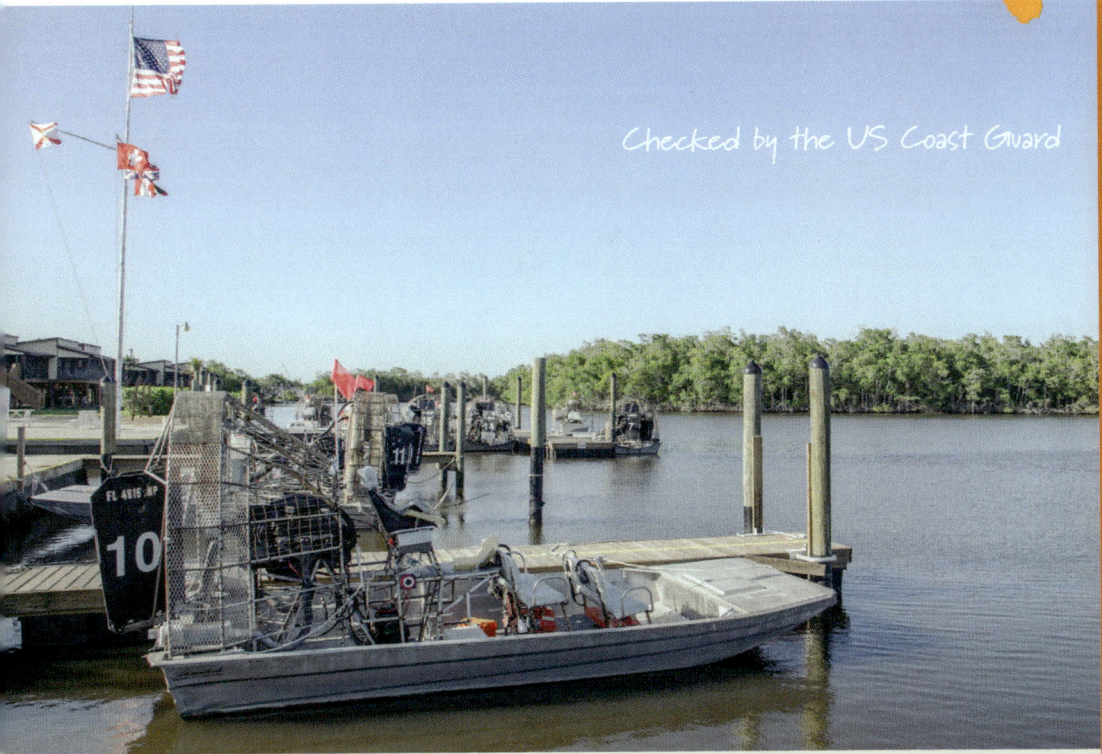

Checked by the US Coast Guard

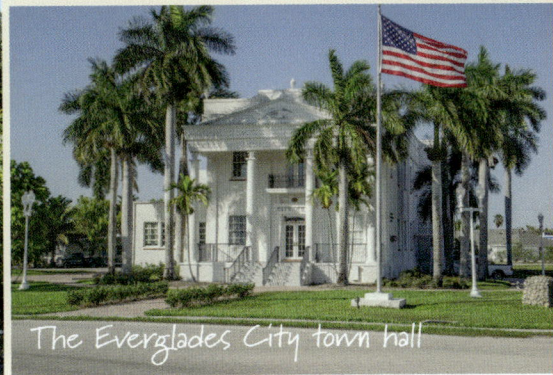

The Everglades City town hall

KFXE

| R W Y | 08-26 • 6002 x 100 ft. *4-light PAPI, left* |
| | 13-31 • 4000 x 100 ft. *2-light PAPI, left* |

ATIS: 119.85
ASOS: ☎ 954-772-2537
Ground: 121.75
Tower: 120.9
Clearance Delivery: 127.95

SERVICE

JET A1, 100LL
Transport: Courtesy cars

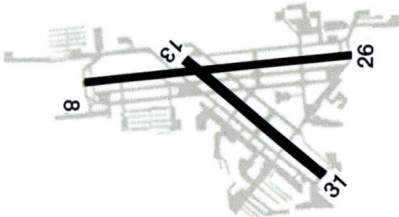

Largest pilot shop in Florida

FORT LAUDERDALE EXECUTIVE AIRPORT

It was 1838 when Major William Lauderdale – who was in the middle of skirmishes with the Seminoles – received the order to build a fort where Fort Lauderdale is now located. The first wooden fort became dilapidated after a time and was followed by two others, both in different areas of today's greater metropolitan area. Nevertheless, it was difficult for a settlement to take hold in this region because the ground was simply too boggy. However, once the city was connected to the railroad by Henry Flagler, artificial canals were built to route the water from the swamp using the excavated soil for reinforcement, the city enjoyed continuous growth and now has 160,000 inhabitants. This clever intervention in nature's natural course gave the city its nickname

Enough room – even for large aircraft

Entrance to the Banyon Pilot Shop

Entrance to the FBO

"Venice of America" and "Yachting Capital of the World." Almost 165 miles of water canals run through the city and have become a definitive part of the cityscape.

Ft. Lauderdale has two major airports. One is the Fort Lauderdale Hollywood International (KFLL) airport and is primarily used by the major airlines while the Fort Lauderdale Executive Airport is mainly used for business flights and private charter planes. There are three major FBOs at the Executive Airport that provide services: **Sano Jet Center**, **World Jet Inc** and **Banyan**. We recommend taxiing directly over to Banyan, which can be reached on runway 13-31 and is relatively easy to find. However, runway 08-26 is also frequently in operation. If you're not sure how to get there, you can request "progressive taxi" on the Ground frequency. This option, which you generally always have, is explicitly carried out in the A/FD.

A visit to Banyan is worth it for two reasons: First, one of the hangars houses Florida's largest pilot store, the Banyan Pilot Shop, and secondly, arguably one of the better airport cafés **Jet Café**, which offers a separate breakfast menu for those who have a very early start. If you make any purchases in the Pilot Shop or refuel at Banyan, you won't have to pay a parking fee for your airplane. Also, Banyan provides courtesy cars that you can use for a quick visit to town or the beach. Please note: Prior to departure and before taxiing, you have to obtain clearance from clearance delivery, only then do you get onto the Ground frequency for taxi clearance. This process is rather unusual for a Class D airport, but is probably due to the high traffic at this airport and the surrounding air space.

KTMB

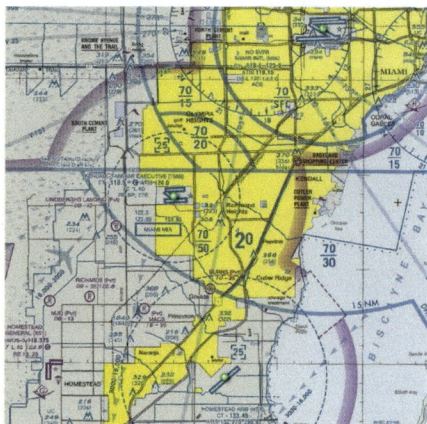

KENDALL-TAMIAMI EXECUTIVE AIRPORT

RWY
09R-27L • 5999 x 150 ft.
09R: 4-light PAPI, right
27L: 4-light PAPI, left

09L-27R • 5003 x 150 ft.
09L: 4-light PAPI, left
27R: 2-light PAPI, left

13-31 • 4001 x 150 ft.
13: 4-light PAPI, left

ATIS: 124.0
ASOS: ☎ 305-235-1332
Ground: 121.7
Tower: 118.9

SERVICE

JET A1, 100LL
Courtesy car, enterprise, AVIS

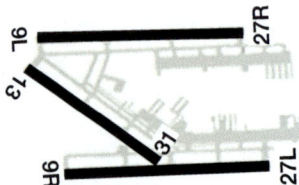

Miami is neither the capital city nor is it the largest city in the Sunshine State, but everyone sure thinks it is. The city's rise began in the 1980's with the drug trade. It is estimated that at that time 80% of all drugs sold in the United States came into the country through Miami. The sheer unimaginable sums of drug money had to be laundered, which was done mainly through the real estate market. Today, Miami boasts one of the most impressive skylines in the United States. However, with vast amounts of drugs, violence and crime also rose. The once sleepy town became one of the most dangerous metropolises in the country. Luckily, this is now all a thing of the past. Today, Miami's prosperity comes from a booming finance industry, trade and tourism. Downtown Miami has the highest concentration of international banks in the United States, higher than even New York. The subtropical climate attracts thousands and thousands of tourists from all over the world each year, intensifying its image as an already heavily diverse multicultural city. Next to El Paso, Texas, Miami has the largest Spanish-speaking population in the United States. Most of the residents in this community have Cuban roots, so it isn't surprising that Little Havana is a major city district that is obviously Cuban in character.

Miami has also made a name for itself as a seaport. The Port of Miami is home to the largest cruise ship harbor in the world. In addition to trade, banking and tourism, the art scene in Miami has grown exponentially in the last few years. In other words, Miami has something for everyone – much more than just the "long, white sandy beaches" of Miami Beach. The Kendall-Tamiami Executive Airport is located in the southwest part of the city and is certainly one of the busiest airports described in this guide. The airport has three FBOs, with **Landmark Aviation** being the largest. It has all the services and facilities that you could possibly need, including pool tables, rental and courtesy cars, though courtesy cars can only be loaned out for a short period of time. Because it takes about 45 minutes to drive into downtown Miami means that it's not worth using a courtesy car. During our last visit, we parked our aircraft at **Reliance Aviation**. Reliance is not as fancy as Landmark, but has all the necessary services you need, including rental cars. If you refuel here, there is no parking fee.

A lot of business aviation

KEYW

R W Y 09-27 • 4801 x 100 ft.
4-box VASI on left

ATIS: 119.675
ASOS: 119.65 (☎ 305-292-4046)
Ground: 121.9
Tower: 118.2

SERVICE

JET A1, 100LL

The Caribbean in America

KEY WEST INTERNATIONAL AIRPORT

A flight to Key West definitely ranks among the high points for pilots in Florida. Caribbean ambience, gorgeous flight over the Keys and a place that even cast its spell

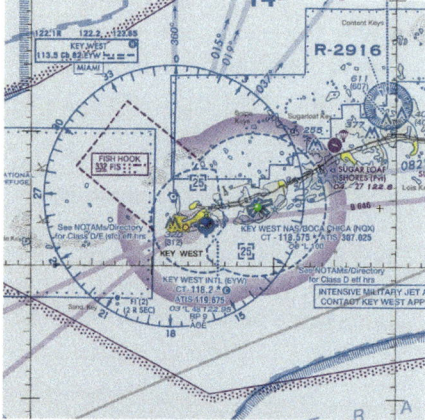

KEYW – Surrounded by water

on the likes of Ernest Hemingway. This and much more make KEYW an interesting destination. Coming from the North, you generally fly along the coastline. However, one controlled air space follows another in quick succession. Air space transitions are usually granted as long as you stay low enough to avoid interfering with take-off and landing traffic. That's why you are often directed to fly at altitudes

between 500 and 1000 ft. If you fly low over the shoreline, there is an outstanding view over the ocean, and you might even see devil rays, whales, and dolphins. You

Key West Oceanside Marina

The city is characterized by its southern architecture

Only 90 miles to Cuba from here.

fly along the Fort Lauderdale and Miami skylines, sometimes lower than the top stories of the skyscrapers and directly over the beach. South of Miami Beach are Fisher Island, Virginia Key and Key Biscaine, the first of the small offshore islands. The northern ridge of the actual Keys begins at about the level of Homestead, which is where Elliott Key and Key Largo are located.

Near Marathon, between Homestead and Key West, is a public airport. After Marathon, you should pay special attention to a restricted area (R-2916), which protects a balloon that is tied to a steel cable and floats at a height of roughly 14,000 ft. If you have good eyes, you'll see the balloon, but you can't see the steel cable unless you're really looking for it. That's why disregarding the restricted area has not only legal consequences, but can also ruin your entire day. Shortly

The cruise ships are taller than the houses

before Key West, you first fly over a Naval Air Station that looks incredibly inviting due to its crossed runways, but unfortunately, it is taboo for civil aircraft. After flying through the Navy air space, you are handed over to the Key West Tower for landing.

Once on the ground in Key West, a relatively inconspicuous FBO awaits you with services that leave nothing to be desired. You can rent a car here either from enterprise or AVIS. For a quick trip to town, it's better to take a taxi (about $15 for two people) and enjoy the 10-minute drive to Duval Street, the epicenter of Key West. At the south end of Duval Street, there is a somewhat bulky buoy that marks the "Southernmost Point of Continental U.S.A." The harbor is located at the north end of the street. There are several inviting cafés and restaurants with a relaxed atmosphere and a great view of the nearby islands, at least as long as a cruise ship is not moored at the pier, which blocks the view.

Key West has many museums, including **Hemingway Museum**, the **Shipwreck Museum**, the **Audubon House and Garden** as well as the **Little White House**, where President Harry S. Truman vacationed. You should check out this gem for aviators: the first office of Pan American World Airways at 301 Whitehead St. What began here in Key West with a promising name, later to become known as Pan Am , became one of the world's leading airlines. Its first flight took off from Key West to Havana in 1927. Located today in the former Pan Am building is **Kelly's Caribbean Bar, Grill & Brewery** with a beautifully shaded courtyard and a diverse menu.

The ocean promenade with cafés and restaurants

KMKY

| R W Y | 17-35 • 5000 x 100 ft. *4-light PAPI, left* |

| (•) | CTAF/UNICOM: 122.8
AWOS: 120.075 (☎ 239-394-8187) |

SERVICE

| ⛽ | JET A1, 100LL |

Transport:
Courtesy car, Taxi,
AVIS ☎ 239-643-6402
enterprise ☎ 800-736-8227
Hertz ☎ 1800-654-3131

Small but outstanding -
the FBO in Marco Island

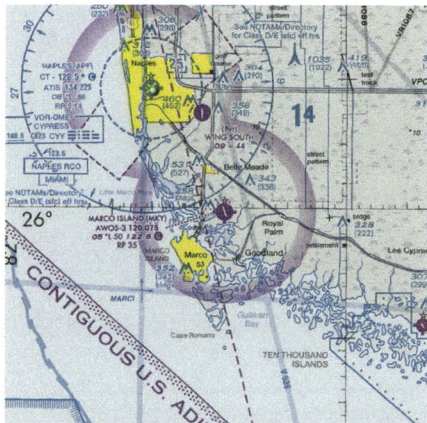

Start of the 10,000 Islands

MARCO ISLAND EXECUTIVE AIRPORT

To avoid confusion, you should know
ahead of time that the Marco Island

Executive Airport is not on Marco Island but rather 11 nm southeast of Naples on the mainland. Marco Island itself is connected to the mainland by a bridge over the Marco River. The airport lies nestled between the **Collier Seminole State Park** and its direct neighbor **Marco Island Resort & Spa** in the middle of the wetlands. The Marco Island Resort & Spa operated by Marriott houses several restaurants as well as a golf course that is open to the public.

Even if you just want to take a short break or enjoy a picnic, there is a small picnic area directly on the water at the north end of the runway. A sign reminds you that you shouldn't feed the alligators.

LINKS

www.themarcoislandprincess.com
www.floridastateparks.org/collierseminole

Marco Island from the traffic pattern

Marco Island itself with its 6,000 inhabitants ranks among one of the more dignified areas on the Gulf Coast. Due to its complex canal system, most of the homes here have direct access to water and even have their own boat landings. This obviously attracts a certain clientele, which is also noticeable about the area. There is a large number of restaurants and cafés to choose from, with something for everyone. It's best to ask at the airport to find out which is the most popular.

If you're interested in combining a boat trip with an outstanding dining experience, then you should think about booking a tour with **Sunshine Tours**. The Marco Island Princess runs daily, taking different routes through the island world. Take in the spectacular views while enjoying a delicious lunch or dinner. You can also just do the sightseeing tour without the meal. Departure: Rose Marina, 951 Bald Eagle Drive, Marco Island, FL.

The Collier Seminole State Park can be reached by car in 20 minutes. A broad array of outdoor recreational activities awaits visitors. There are walking trails, a short mountain bike trail as well as many fishing options. For those eager to get on the water, you can rent a canoe or kayak for several hours and explore the islands at your leisure. The animal world here is very diverse, with many bird species, manatees, panthers, rattlesnakes, otters, raccoons and, of course, the ever-present alligator. Do not forget mosquito repellent!

To get to the island or the state park, rental cars from enterprise, Hertz and Avis are available. I recommend doing this because courtesy car availability is somewhat limited.

Airport from the traffic pattern

The runway is long enough for larger aircraft

BE
AWARE
OF
ALLIGATORS

PLEASE
DO NOT
FEED THE
ANIMALS

Picnic area for aviators and alligators

141

KAPF

NAPLES
MUNICIPAL
AIRPORT

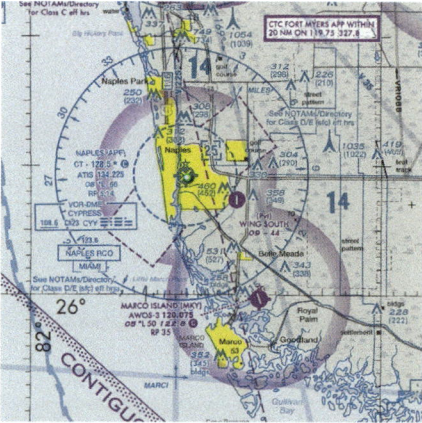

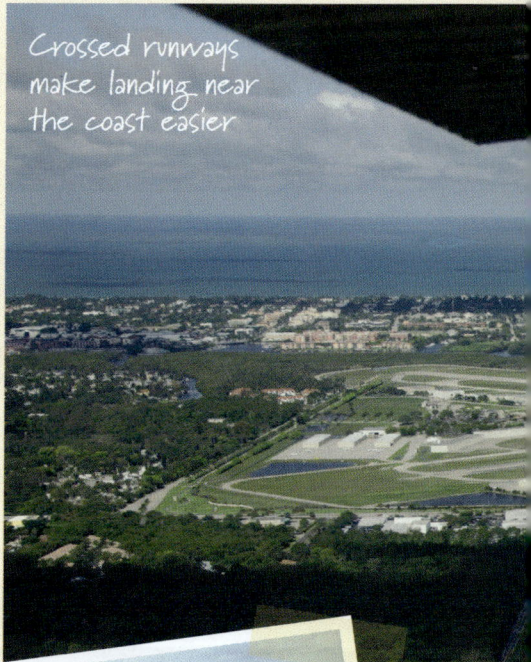

Crossed runways make landing near the coast easier

RWY
05-23 • 6600 x 150 ft.
05: 4-light PAPI, right
23: 4-light PAPI, left

14-23 • 5000 x 100 ft.
4-light PAPI, left

Ground: 121.6
Tower: 128.5
ATIS: 134.225

SERVICE

JET A1, 100LL

Transport: Crew Car, Taxi, enterprise, Hertz, AVIS

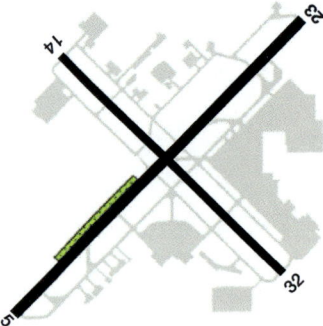

Built on the water

Naples Municipal Airport is just a few minutes by car from downtown. The crossed runways make landing easier and the FBO's fantastic service takes care of the rest. If you refuel here, you can park your plane free of charge and are offered a courtesy car for 1.5 hours. Otherwise, the parking fee is $21.

Even if Naples doesn't have Vesuvius, this city on the Gulf of Mexico still exudes a Mediterranean feel. Skyscrapers are huddled together at the north end

of town, while the downtown has low rises and a long white sandy beach. The city has 22,000 inhabitants, though this number rises considerably in the winter. Naples is frequently called Palm Beach's little sister on the Gulf. You have to have a good income to live here. Either during the approach or the take-off, you shouldn't miss flying along the coast at a lower altitude to enjoy a fantastic view of the mansions and gardens.

If you drive into town using the crew car and have limited time, it's best to drive to Naples pier. Like most port cities, life centers around the water.

For eating and shopping, I recommend **Tin City** (1200 5th Avenue South Naples, FL 34102). Here, right on the water, you will find a large selection of shops and several good restaurants that leave nothing to be desired. My favorites are **Riverwalk** and **Pinchers Crab Shack**. Right near the airport and popular among pilots is **Michelbobs**, a BBQ restaurant famous for its spare ribs. However, check the website for its business hours, they vary depending on the season. It's best to ask at the FBO or to check their website (see below). **Alice Sweetwater** an **Joes Diner** are good alternatives.

If the crew car is not available or you want more time, car rental companies enterprise, Hertz and AVIS have offices in the FBO.

SIGHTSEEING

Naples Museum of Art
Naples Depot Museum
Collier County Museum

LINKS

www.michelbobs.com
www.alicesweetwatersbarandgrille.com

The greater Naples area is
famous for its gardens

KOBE

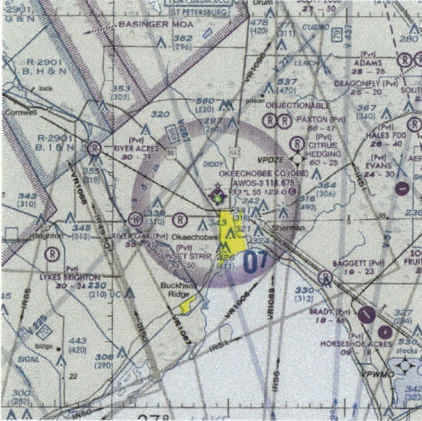

OKEECHOBEE COUNTY AIRPORT

Lake Okeechobee or Big O, as the locals affectionately call it, is the largest freshwater lake in Florida. Covering almost 730 sq miles, it is three times as large as Lake Constance and the seventh largest freshwater lake in the United States.

R W Y
05-23 • 5000 x 100 ft.
05: 4-light PAPI, right
23: 4-light PAPI, left
14-32 • 4001 x 75 ft.
4-light PAPI, left

CTAF/UNICOM: 123.0
AWOS: 118.675

SERVICE

JET A1, 100LL

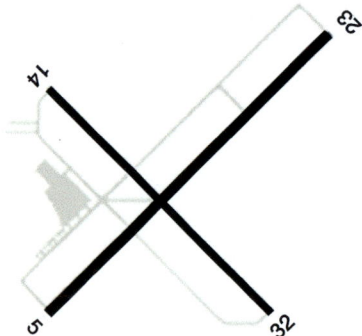

The Landing Strip Café – this is where you have the best view

Due to its geographical location, the Okeechobee County Airport is a typical domestic airport that is a popular food and refuel stopover for flights heading further south or returning north. There is not much to see or do near the airport. However, Okeechobee itself is popular among fishermen.

The **Okeechobee Jet Center** is an excellent FBO with friendly and helpful staff that have everything you need for flight planning.

The **Landing Strip Café** directly at the airport offers traditional American-style meals.

You can park directly in front of the café and watch the flight action while enjoying your meal.

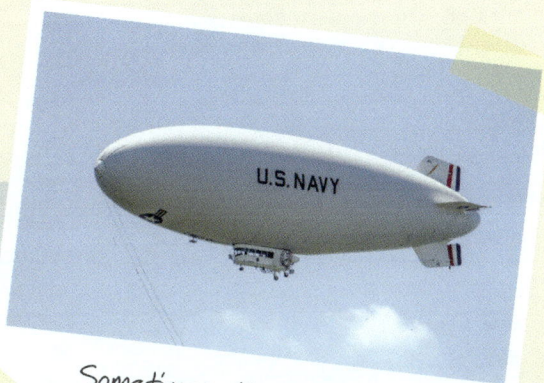

Sometimes, the Navy also stops by

The runway is also long enough for larger aircraft

KFMY

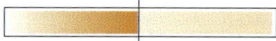

R W Y	05-23 • 6406 x 150 ft.
	4-box VASI, left
	13-31 • 4912 x 150 ft.
	4-box VASI, left

ATIS: 123.725
ASOS: ☎ 239-936-2318
Ground: 121.7
Tower: 119.0

SERVICE

JET A1, 100LL
Transport: Courtesy car, Hertz

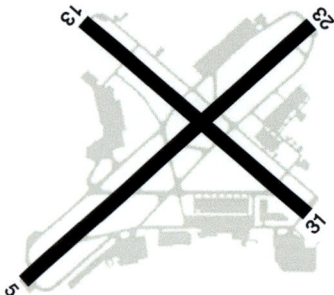

Ready for the Island?

PAGE FIELD AIRPORT, FORT MYERS

Fort Myers has 62,000 inhabitants and is one of the largest cities on Florida's west coast. The city was named after the military post that was founded there in 1850 during skirmishes with the Seminole tribe. Later, Ft. Myers was made famous by a certain Thomas Alva Edison who invented the light bulb here. Today Ft. Myers is a magnet for wealthy retirees who move to this area to enjoy their retirement years - which is not unusual in Florida. What also makes Ft. Myers interesting are the nearby Sanibel Island and Captiva Island. Sanibel Island can be reached fastest. It has no fast food restaurants or large shopping centers and not even any skyscrapers. Very early on in its history, the city council decided that no house or building could be higher than the highest palm tree.

I recommend renting a car for the entire day. It's worth it. You could use a courtesy car free of charge, but it's only available for 2 hours, which is not a lot of time for exploring the island. It's also about a half-hour drive just to get there. However, for about $50-60, you can get a car for the entire day. You have to take the toll road ($6 round-trip) and go over the bridge, opened in 1963, to Sanibel. The island is particularly popular among sea shell collectors. Each year, more shells are washed up on shore than at any other place in the United States. The beaches are just covered with them especially after a storm. If you have no luck in collecting shells and still want to take home some nice ones as souvenirs, go visit **She Sells Sea Shells**.

Passionate shell collectors meet in Sanibel every March for the

LINKS

www.shellmuseum.org
www.billysrentals.com

Exterior of the FBO

Sanibel Shell Festival. If you want a quick overview of the variety of shells, then try visiting the Bailey -Matthews Shell Museum (3075 Sanibel-Captiva Road, Sanibel, FL 33957, Tel.: +1 (239-395-2233). It has more than 400 types of different shells to marvel at.

Sanibel does have more than shells to offer, you can also see dolphins right from the beach, though the best place is at Lighthouse Beach.

Also, both Sanibel and Captiva Islands are home to the Loggerhead turtles und the Gopher Tortoise which are in danger of extinction. They lay their eggs here in August. Loggerhead turtles are ocean turtles between 1 and 1.5 m long and up to 150 kg in weight.

RESTAURANTS I recommend **The Timbers Restaurant & Fish Market**, 703 Tarpon Bay Road, Sanibel, FL 33957. Timbers has established itself as an outstanding restaurant for fish and oysters in the last few years.

Gramma Dot's Seaside, 634 N Yachtman Drive, Sanibel, FL 33957. Here, you can enjoy the maritime ambience directly at the Sanibel Marina with a view of the hips and the water.

Parked in the shade

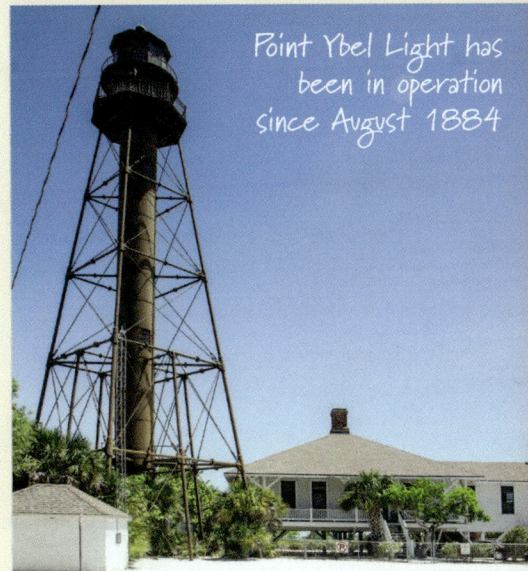
Point Ybel Light has been in operation since August 1884

Billy's Rentals (1470 Periwinkle Way Sanibel, FL 33957) rents bicycles, Vespas and Segways so you can explore the island and its 35 km trail system at your own speed.

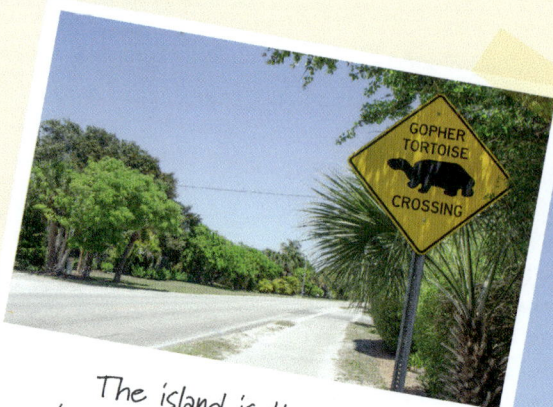

The island is the breeding ground for the threatened Georgia gopher tortoise.

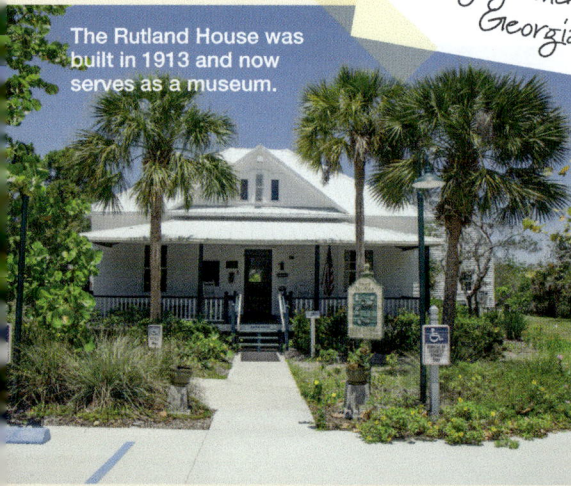

The Rutland House was built in 1913 and now serves as a museum.

The name says it all.

Dolphins can be seen
from the beach

Sanibel Marina
with Gramma
Dot's Restaurant

KLNA

R W Y	09-27 • 3489 x 75 ft.
	15-33 • 3421 x 100 ft.
	03-21 • 3256 x 75 ft.

CTAF/UNICOM: 122.7
AWOS: 119.925 (☎ 561-964-0308)

SERVICE

JET A1, 100LL

PBFC Local Yellow Cab
☎ +1 561-474-2222
☎ +1 561-578-3322 (Mobil)
or All Transportations Taxi
☎ +1 561-450-5858

It's pretty relaxed here

Beach and luxury

PALM BEACH COUNTY PARK AIRPORT (LANTANA)

About 5 nm south of Palm Beach International is the considerably smaller Palm Beach County Park Airport – or also called Lantana Airport, named after the area where it is located. When approaching from the west, pay attention to the antennas that are very high at 1599 ft and are located just under the KPBI air space. The airport itself offers little worth mentioning: three runways, a small FBO, several waiting areas, a flight school and sufficient parking. Nevertheless, it is the first choice for those wanting to see Palm Beach, but who do not want to fly into hectic Palm Beach International. (Although VFR traffic is handled in KPBI, the short runway 10R/28L is mainly used for this purpose.)

Long before Miami became as big and prestigious as it is today, Palm Beach was the winter refuge for the rich and the beautiful in Florida. Palm Beach itself consists of two very different city districts: West Palm Beach, the busy business center, and real Palm Beach, with its luxury mansions, expensive shopping malls, cafés and restaurants. Those wanting to swim at Palm Beach and don't own their own piece of beach head north to Jupiter Beach.

Considerably closer to Lantana are the beaches of Lake Worth. It's a 10-minute taxi ride to the **Lake Worth Casino**

Building & Beach Complex. This facility has white sandy beaches that go for miles. The water here is shallow and warm. The casino, which is still called a casino only for historical reasons, has a good menu with sandwiches or snacks to fill you up before the return flight. A genuine attraction in Lantana is the **Old Key Lime House** which is now home to a restaurant that I highly recommend. The building itself was built in 1889 and was fully restored at the turn of the last century when it was turned into a restaurant. Today, it is proudly called the "Oldest Waterfront Restaurant in Florida." You can sit and enjoy the rustic and tropical ambience indoors or take a table on the water and enjoy the wonderful view of the Intracoastal Waterway. The front part of the building is a bar while the back is a restaurant - each area has different menus. There is live music here on the weekends.

One of the two large antennas in the approach area

KMTH

R W Y	07-25 • 5008 x 100 ft. *4-light PAPI, left*

((•))	CTAF/UNICOM: 122.8 AWOS: 135.525 (☎ 305-743-8373)

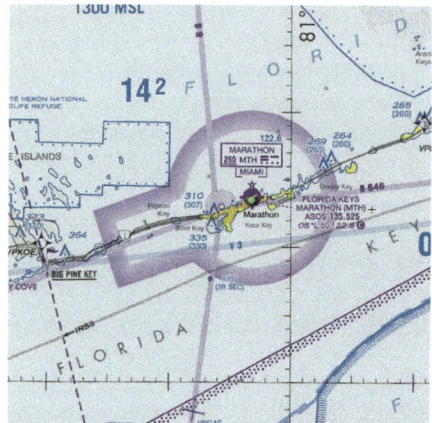

SERVICE

⛽	JET A1, 100LL

Transport:
AVIS ☎ 305-743-5428
Budget ☎ 305-743-3998
enterprise ☎ 305-289-7630
Courtesy cars

More than just a stopover

THE FLORIDA KEYS MARA-THON AIRPORT

What looks on the map like a small sleepy town on the way to Key West is actually a relatively busy airport, even if uncontrolled. Its runway length appears more suitable for business jets. The truth is that the runway in Marathon is longer than the one at Key West International, which

seems remarkable. However, Marathon is frequently used as the jump-off point for harder-to-reach resorts. Visitors are flown out from here by helicopter. Nevertheless, there is enough air traffic for two FBOs that share the business. **Marathon Jet Center** at the west end of the runway handles jets, as the name implies, and **Marathon General Aviation** on the east end of the runway handles piston engine business.

There is no restaurant at the airport itself. Both FBOs, however, offer beverages and snacks. If you're looking for a proper meal, then you'll need to order a taxi or rent a car.

There are many restaurants to choose from, the nearest of which is the **Fish Tales Market & Eatery**, 11711 Overseas Highway Marathon, FL 33050, Tel.: (305) 743-9196. This restaurant is appealing because of its proximity to the airport. **Keys Fisheries Market & Marina**, 3502 Gulfview Avenue, Marathon, FL 33050, Tel.: 305-743-4353 can be reached in just a few minutes by taxi and is located directly on the water.

LINKS

www.keysfisheries.com
www.floridalobster.com

KVNC

VENICE MUNICIPAL AIRPORT

Venice is one of the wealthier cities on Florida's Gulf Coast. The average age of its approx. 20,000 inhabitants is 69. Many retirees move to Venice to enjoy their twilight years. That's why low approaches over town should be avoided if at all possible. Make sure you use right traffic pattern for runway 13.

Other than its proximity to the water, there is not much to do in Venice. However, the city fathers have gone to great efforts to endow Venice with a Mediterranean flair. Venice Municipal Airport is located between the Intracoastal Waterway and the beach. Runway 05-23 starts and ends almost on the beach. Tightly nestled between runway 13-31 and the beach is the **Lake Venice Golf Course**. If you want to refuel at Suncoast or enjoy a meal at the Suncoast Café, you will not be charged the $10 parking fee. The airport café is certainly not a bad solution if you are in a hurry, but when it comes to quality and ambience as well

RWY
05-23 • 5000 x 150 ft.
13-31 • 4999 x 150 ft.
13: 2-light PAPI, left
31: 4-light PAPI, left

CTAF/UNICOM: 122.725
AWOS: 119.275

SERVICE

A1, 100LL
Rental cars: enterprise
Taxi: Organized by the FBO.

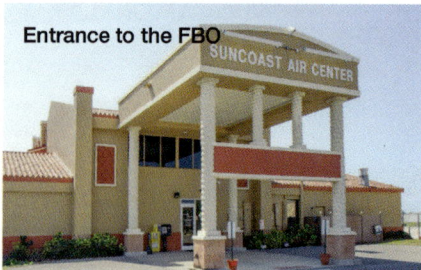

Entrance to the FBO

as other attractions, it cannot keep up with Venice. Far better, within walking distance and directly on the beach, is one of the most popular eateries among local pilots – **Sharky's On the Pier**. Sharkys has an outstanding selection of seafood and first-class cocktails. With a Caribbean atmosphere, you can sit on the pier with your feet in the sand and a view of the water.

It takes about 25-minutes to walk to Sharky's from the **Suncoast FBO** (Texaco is closer) or you can call the Sharky's Shuttle from the FBO, which runs

customers between the restaurant and the FBO starting around 11:30 a.m. well into the evening. South of Sharky's is **Caspersen Beach** where you might find fossilized shark teeth, if you're lucky. This is where Venice gets its nickname "The Shark Tooth Capital."

TIP Enjoy sunset with a Sundowner on the deck at Sharky's.

Sharky's - popular among fishermen and aviators

Waiting for the big fish...

LINKS

www.lakevenicegolf.com
www.sharkysonthepier.com

The pier right in front of Sharky's

KVRB

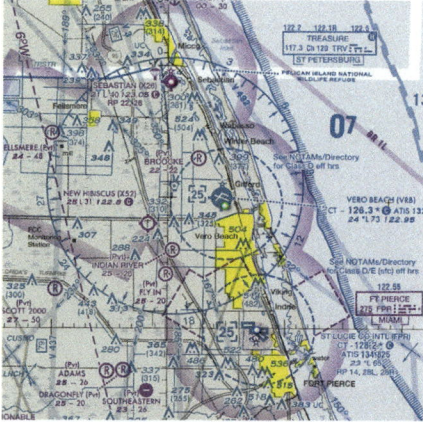

R W Y	11R-29L • 7314 x 100 ft. *4-light PAPI, left* 11L-29R • 3504 x 75 ft. *2-light PAPI, left* 04-22 • 4974 x 100 ft. *04: 4-box VASI, left* *22: 4-light PAPI, left*

ATIS: 132.5
ASOS: ☎ 772-978-9535
Ground: 127.45
Tower: 126.3
Clearance Delivery: 134.975

SERVICE

JET A, 100LL

VERO BEACH MUNICIPAL AIRPORT

Aviators undoubtedly associate the name Vero Beach with the name **Piper Aircraft**. Its Vero Beach production facility is where the company chose to consolidate its business operations, bringing together its research and development activities, its production and sales as well as maintenance work for all aircraft. The good news is that Piper offers regular tours of the production plant that are worth it for anyone interested in how a Piper aircraft is built. After a brief history of the Piper plant, you can watch how an airplane is slowly and safely built, starting with the first metal parts and rivets. As a rule, the Piper tour is led by retired Piper staff who know the company's entire history and have many anecdotes to

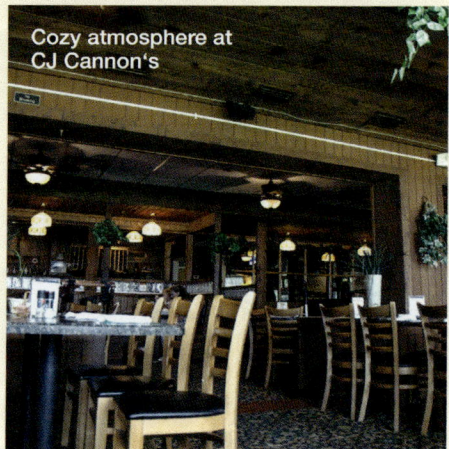

Cozy atmosphere at CJ Cannon's

tell. They leave no question un-
answered. Tours are held on Tues
and Thurs at 10:00 a.m. and 1:00
p.m. You should register beforehand and wear sturdy shoes. Tel.:
772-299-2820, Piper Aircraft, 2926
Piper Drive, Vero Beach, FL 32960.
The distance from the FBO to the
entrance of the Piper building is walkable.

The airport here is also home to
one of the most famous restaurants
in Florida, **CJ Cannon's**. It has been
around for 30 years and its history
is reflected on the walls of the restaurant.

If you're looking for culinary classics, you won't be disappointed.
The prices are reasonable, the
service friendly and the food is
excellent – a perfect recipe
for the next 30 years of success!

The airport entrance is just a few meters away from Piper.

Mirage prior to delivery

BIBLIOGRAPHY

1 National Historic Landmarks Program, Windover Archeological Site:
http://tps.cr.nps.gov/nhl/detail.cfm?ResourceId=1980&ResourceType=Site,
http://en.wikipedia.org/wiki/Windover_archaeological_site

2 "Archaic Shell Rings from the Southeast U.S. National Historic Landmarks. Historic Context." Southeast Archeological Center, National Park Service, Tallahassee, 2002. http://www.nps.gov/nhl/themes/Archaic%20Shell%20Rings.pdf

3 Milanich, Jerald T. Florida's Indians From Ancient Time to the Present. University Press of Florida. 1998.

4 Brown, Ian (2003). "Introduction to the Bottle Creek Site" In Brown, Ian W. Bottle Creek, A Pensacola Culture Site in South Alabama. Tuscaloosa: University of Alabama Press.

5 Fogelson, Raymond D., Vol. Ed. Handbook of North American Indians, Vol. 14: Southeast. Smithsonian Institution. 2004.

6 Jerald T. Milanich, „What happened to the Timucua Indians?", AAA Native Arts Gallery

7 Seminole Nation of Oklahoma
http://sno-nsn.gov/culture/aboutsno
http://en.wikipedia.org/wiki/Seminole_Nation_of_Oklahoma

8 Seminole Tribe of Florida
http://www.semtribe.com/
http://en.wikipedia.org/wiki/Seminole_Tribe_of_Florida

9 Miccosukee Tribe of Indians of Florida
http://www.miccosukeetribe.com/

http://en.wikipedia.org/wiki/Miccosukee_Tribe_of_Indians_of_Florida
10 Gonzalo Fernández de Oviedo. Historia General y Natural de las Indias, Parte I (1535), Libro 16, capítulo XI. http://www.ems.kcl.ac.uk/content/etext/e026.html#d0e8753

11 Smith, Hale G. and Marc Gottlob. 1978. "Spanish-Indian Relationships: Synoptic History and Archaeological Evidence, 1500-1763," in Tacachale: Essays on the Indians of Florida and Southeastern Georgia during the Historic Period, by Milanich, Jerald and Samuel Proctor. Gainesville, Florida: The University Presses of Florida.

12 Pánfilo de Narváez, http://en.wikipedia.org/wiki/P%C3%A1nfilo_de_Narv%C3%A1ez
13 The disaster of these early journeys of exploration were retold by Álvar Núñez Cabeza de Vaca in Naufragios.

14 Hernando de Soto, http://en.wikipedia.org/wiki/Hernando_de_Soto_(explorer)

15 Bense, Judith Ann (1999). Archaeology of Colonial Pensacola (1999 ed.). University Press of Florida.

16 Pensacola, history http://en.wikipedia.org/wiki/Pensacola#History

17 Rowland, Lawrence Sanders; Moore, Alexander ;Rogers, George C. The History of Beaufort County, South Carolina: 1514–1861 (1996 ed.). University of South Carolina Press.

18 Pedro Menéndez de Aviléz, http://en.wikipedia.org/wiki/Pedro_Men%C3%A9ndez_de_Avil%C3%A9s

19 Gallay, Alan. The Indian Slave Trade: The Rise of the English Empire in the American South,

1670–1717. Yale University Press. 2002.

20 Miller, E: "St. Augustine's British Years," page 38. The Journal of the St. Augustine Historical Society, 2001.

21 Mahon, John K.; Brent R. Weisman (1996). "Florida's Seminole and Miccosukee Peoples" In Gannon, Michael (Ed.). The New History of Florida, pp. 183–206. University Press of Florida. 22 Treaty of Paris http://www.ourdocuments.gov/doc.php?flash=true&doc=6

23 Treaty of San Lorenzo http://en.wikipedia.org/wiki/Treaty_of_San_Lorenzo

24 Republic of West Florida, http://en.wikipedia.org/wiki/Republic_of_West_Florida

25 Louisana Purchase, Original Treaty, http://www.archives.gov/exhibits/american_originals/louistxt.html

26 West Florida, Annexation of territories http://en.wikipedia.org/wiki/West_Florida#American_annexation_of_the_territory

27 First Seminole War - http://en.wikipedia.org/wiki/First_Seminole_War#First_Seminole_War

28 Adams-Onís Treaty, http://en.wikipedia.org/wiki/Adams-On%C3%ADs_Treaty

29 Florida Territory, http://en.wikipedia.org/wiki/Florida_Territory

30 Treaty of Payne's Landing - http://en.wikipedia.org/wiki/Treaty_of_Payne%27s_Landing Historical document - http://www.johnhorse.com/trail/02/a/06.1.htm

31 Dade Massacre - http://www.dadebattlefield.com/ http://en.wikipedia.org/wiki/Dade_Massacre

32 Third Seminole War - http://en.wikipedia.org/wiki/Third_Seminole_War#Third_Seminole_War

33 American Civil War - http://en.wikipedia.org/wiki/American_Civil_War

35 Reconstruction Era - http://en.wikipedia.org/wiki/Reconstruction_Era

36 Disfranchisement after the Reconstruction Era - http://en.wikipedia.org/wiki/Disfranchisement_after_the_Reconstruction_Era

37 Jim Crow Laws - http://en.wikipedia.org/wiki/Jim_Crow_laws

38 African American % of population - http://en.wikipedia.org/wiki/List_of_U.S._states_by_African-American_population#African-American_.25_of_Population_.281790-2010.29_by_U.S._State

39 Rosewood Massacre - http://www.ghosttowns.com/states/fl/rosewood.html http://www.displaysforschools.com/rosewoodrp.html

40 The Great Migration - http://en.wikipedia.org/wiki/Great_Migration_(African_American)

41 Henry Flagler - http://en.wikipedia.org/wiki/Henry_Flagler

42 Hotel Ponce de León in St. Augustine - http://en.wikipedia.org/wiki/Hotel_Ponce_de_Leon

43 Hotel Poinciana and Breakers Hotel http://royalpoincianahotel.blogspot.ch/

44 Sunken Gardens - http://en.wikipedia.org/wiki/Sunken_Gardens_(Florida)

45 Silver Springs - http://en.wikipedia.org/wiki/Silver_Springs,_Florida

46 Weeki Wachee Springs - http://en.wikipedia.org/wiki/Weeki_Wachee_Springs

47 Cypress Gardens - http://en.wikipedia.org/wiki/Cypress_Gardens

48 Marineland - http://en.wikipedia.org/wiki/Marineland_of_Florida

49 Mormino, Gary R. Land of Sunshine, State of Dreams: A Social History of Modern Florida. Gainesville: University Press of Florida, 2005.

50 Indians-Gambling-Revenues... http://articles.sun-sentinel.com/2013-02-27/business/fl-indians-gambling-revenues-022713-20130227_1_alan-meister-indian-casinos-table-games

51 Walt Disney World - http://en.wikipedia.org/wiki/Walt_Disney_World

52 SeaWorld - http://en.wikipedia.org/wiki/Seaworld#SeaWorld_Orlando

53 Universal Studios Florida - http://en.wikipedia.org/wiki/Universal_Studios_Florida

54 Walt Disney World, Employment http://en.wikipedia.org/wiki/Walt_Disney_World#Employment

55 Orlando International Airport http://en.wikipedia.org/wiki/Orlando_International_Airport

56 Demographics of Florida - http://www.npg.org/states/fl.htm http://en.wikipedia.org/wiki/Demographics_of_Florida

57 Carl Graham Fisher - http://en.wikipedia.org/wiki/Carl_Fisher

58 Idem

59 Hendricks Army Airfield - http://en.wikipedia.org/wiki/Sebring_Regional_Airport

60 Sebring International Raceway -http://www.sebringraceway.com/

61 GI Bill - http://en.wikipedia.org/wiki/Gi_bill

62 Mormino, Gary R. Land of Sunshine...

63 Naval Air Station Pensacola - http://en.wikipedia.org/wiki/Naval_Air_Station_Pensacola

64 Eglin Air Force Base - http://en.wikipedia.org/wiki/Naval_Air_Station_Pensacola

65 Orlando Air Force Base - http://en.wikipedia.org/wiki/Orlando_Air_Force_Base

66 MacDill Air Force Base - http://en.wikipedia.org/wiki/Macdill_Air_Force_Base

67 Avon Park Air Force Range - http://en.wikipedia.org/wiki/Avon_Park_Air_Force_Range

PHOTO CREDITS

Photo, page 29: Henry Flagler House
Roger Wollstadt from Sarasota, Florida

Photo, page 30:
Weeki Wachee Springs State Park, Florida
Leonard J. DeFrancisci

Photo, page 31: Schild Sunken Gardens
Ebyabe

Photo, page 31: Catalpa tree, Sunken Gardens
Ssriram mt

ABBREVIATIONS

ADIZ	Air Defense Identification Zone
AFD	Airport Facility Directory
AIM	Aeronautical Information Manual
ASOS	Automatic Service Observation System
ATC	Air Traffic Control
ATIS	Automated Terminal Information Service
AWOS	Automated Weather Observation System
BFR	Biennial Flight Review
CFI	Certified Flight Instructor
CFII	Certified Flight Instructor Instrument
CTAF	Common Traffic Advisory Frequency
FBO	Fixed Base Operator
FIS	Flight information services
FSDO	Flight Standard District Office
GNG	Ground
HIWAS	Hazardous In Flight Weather Advisory Service
METAR	Meteorological Terminal Aviation Routine Weather Report
MOA	Military Operation Area
NOTAM	Notice to Airmen
OAT	Outside air temperature
PAPI	Precision Approach Path Indicator
PIC	Pilot in Command
PIREP	Pilot Report
SQL	Squelch
TAF	Terminal area forecast
TCAS	Traffic collision avoidance system
TFR	Temporary Flight Restriction
TRACON	Terminal radar approach control
TWR	Tower
UNICOM	Universal Communications
VASI	Visual Approach Slope Indicator
XPDR	Transponder

INDEX

THANK YOU!

My warmest thanks goes to my
better half Carola and my daughters
Pernille and Junnie for their patience
and understanding. I'd like to also
thank Isabel Brücher for her
article on the history of Florida
and Melanie Ellmers-Ost and
Silke Diekmann for their help with
text and graphic layout. Without their good taste, their patience
and their loving attention to detail,
this book would never have made
it this far. I'd also like to express
my gratitude to the editorial team
at *fliegermagazin* for their encourage-
ment, support and trust.

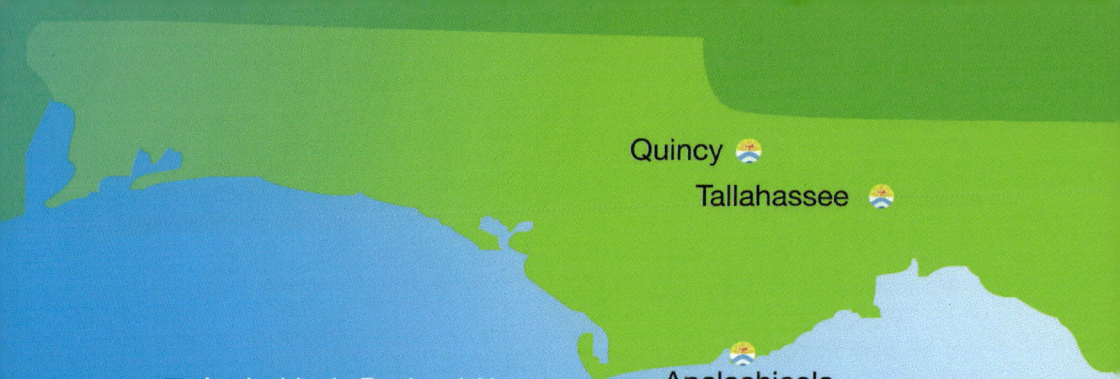

Quincy 🏖

Tallahassee 🏖

Apalachicola 🏖
Apalachicola

- Apalachicola Regional Airport
- Cedar Key - George T Lewis Airport
- Gainesville
- Jekyll Island, GA
- Lake City Gateway Airport
- Quincy
- St. Augustine - Northeast Florida Regional Airport
- St. Simons - Malcolm Mc Kinnon Airport, GA
- Tallahassee Regional Airport
- Williston Municipal Airport

- Albert Whitted Airport, St. Petersburg
- Chalet Suzanne
- Crystal River
- Deland Municipal-Sidney H Taylor Field Airport
- Flagler County Airport
- Inverness Airport
- Kissimmee Gateway Airport
- Lakeland Linder Regional Airport
- Mid Florida Air Service Airport
- New Smyrna Beach Municipal Airport
- Ocala Intl Airport Jim Taylor Field
- Plant City Airport
- River Ranch Resort Airport
- Spruce Creek
- Titusville - Space Coast Regional Airport
- Winter Haven Municipal Airport Gilbert Field
- Zephyrhills Municipal Airport

- Everglades Airpark, Everglades City
- Fort Lauderdale Executive Airport
- Kendall-Tamiami Executive Airport
- Key West International Airport
- Marco Island Executive Airport
- Naples Municipal Airport
- Okeechobee County Airport
- Page Field Airport, Fort Myers
- Palm Beach County Park Airport
- The Florida Keys Marathon Airport
- Venice Municipal Airport
- Vero Beach Municipal Airport

FLORIDA

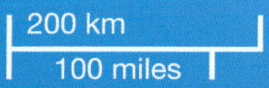

200 km

100 miles

Current information and
tips on flying in Florida
can be found under
www.aviators-guide.com
For more information
and current projects
from Seair Verlag,
please visit
www.seair-verlag.de

SEAIR VERLAG

ISBN-10: 1493504428
ISBN-13: 978-1493504428

14112046R10105

Printed in Great Britain
by Amazon.co.uk, Ltd.,
Marston Gate.